Beyond *Overwhelmed*

FINDING FREEDOM IN MOTHERHOOD

Beyond
Overwhelmed

FINDING FREEDOM IN MOTHERHOOD

Wisdom B. Fields

Copyright © Wisdom B. Fields 2025

All rights reserved. No part of this publication may be reproduced, stored in a retrieval system, or transmitted in any form or by any means, electronic, mechanical, photocopying, recording, or otherwise without prior written permission from the author.

For permission requests, contact
WisdomBFields@gmail.com

ISBN 978-1-7360765-2-1 (Paperback)
ISBN 978-1-7360765-3-8 (ebook)

To my eldest son, thank you for always pushing me to become a better mother and leader. You are complex, unique, and inspiring. It is because of you that I wrote this book.

To my only daughter, I watch with fascination as you share your insights, creativity, and talents. I hope your gift for storytelling opens the door to your dreams.

To my younger son, I continue to be amazed by you. You are a warm and caring soul. You have shown us that with hard work and perseverance, nothing will stand in your way.

This book is dedicated to you, my children. I hope you have learned as many great things from me as I have learned from each one of you. I thank you and will love you forever.

Mom

Contents

Preface ix

INTRODUCTION **The Life You Are Meant to Live** 1

PART I Ground Rules 7

1 **Parent the Child You Have**
   Loosen the reins, so they can discover their own path 9

2 **Let Them Struggle, Let Them Grow**
   If you knock down every hurdle,
   they'll never learn to jump 19

3 **Raising Doers, Not Dependents**
   Teach Them to Fish—
   and Then Step Away from the Shore 31

PART II Self-transformation 45

4 **Mind Games**
   Control Your Mind Before It Control Takes of You 47

5 **Your Journey, Your Way**
   Don't shrink your dreams to fit someone else's fears 59

6 **Leading From Within**
   Inner Power Is Stronger Than Willpower 67

7 **Expanding Perspective**
*When you let go of being right, you begin
to see more clearly* 81

8 **Defusing Conflict**
If You're Strong on the Inside, There's No Need to Fight ... 93

9 **Faith in What Will Be**
*Disappointment Breeds Discouragement,
Faith Offers Hope* 109

10 **Embracing Miracles**
The Improbable Becomes Possible Once You Believe 123

11 **Love in Everything**
Let Love Be the Power Directing Your Light 137

PART III Launch and Discover Your Life Purpose 155

12 **Letting Go, Without Giving Up**
Boundaries Protect You and Move Them Forward 157

13 **Uncovering Purpose**
*The World Will Embrace You When You Know
Who You Are* 173

CONCLUSION **Strengthen Your Core,
the Rest Will Follow** 185

References and Resources 191

About the Author 193

Preface

There's a story I would like to tell—about a queen trying to get her first-born son to leave the comfort of the castle and forge a life of his own. He dreams of ruling distant lands, but he's hesitant to step onto the battlefield. The queen, once sure of herself, begins to doubt. Her other subjects ignore her guidance. The king shakes his head, frustrated, and urges her to fix what feels unfixable. The kingdom's wise men offer all kinds of advice on *what* to do—but it's up to her to figure out *how*.

This isn't a story from Camelot. It's a story from inside a very real home—one that might look a lot like yours. It's a story of a mother doing her best, learning as she goes, and discovering that the only way forward isn't by trying harder to control—but by finding her own strength to lead.

I didn't set out to write a book. I started journaling to make sense of what I was going through—parenting three kids, feeling pressure from all sides, and trying to reconcile the life I imagined with the reality I was living. I'm not a psychologist, therapist, or parenting expert. My degrees are from MIT and Stanford, but my greatest education has come from the messy, beautiful, often overwhelming experience of motherhood. And as a trained co-active coach, I've seen firsthand how many other women are quietly facing similar struggles in a world that often demands perfection while providing little real support.

At first, I thought I was writing to explain my choices—to justify what I was doing and maybe get a little validation. But somewhere along the way, something shifted. I realized this wasn't just about parenting. It was about *me*—the woman I was becoming in the fire of motherhood, being shaped and sharpened in the process. It became clear that **the only way to truly help my children become their best selves was to step into my own power first.**

The greatest impact I could make as a mother wasn't by controlling outcomes or perfecting strategies—it was by reclaiming my own strength. When I began focusing inward rather than outward, I stopped being crushed by disobedience, disappointment, or disapproval. I stopped defending, and started *leading*—with clarity, resilience, and self-trust.

This book is the result of that journey. It's a series of reflections and lessons not just on parenting, but on self-awareness, relationship-building, and growing into the mother—and woman—you're meant to be. Parenting will stretch you in ways nothing else can. It's frustrating, disorienting, and humbling. But it's also an invitation to transform.

If you've ever felt alone, judged, overwhelmed, or unsure of your worth in this role—you're not broken. You're becoming. And in that process, there's opportunity: to reset, to realign, and to rise.

This book isn't about perfection. It's about progress. It's about awareness, honesty, healing, and hope. It's about finding your footing when everything feels shaky, and discovering that the strength you've been searching for? It's been inside you all along.

My hope is that what's written here resonates with mothers everywhere—those who are doing the best they can, who sometimes feel like they're failing, but who are actually in the middle of becoming the strongest, truest versions of themselves.

This is more than a story. It's an invitation—to awaken the power within.

INTRODUCTION
The Life You Are Meant to Live

When the Dalai Lama was asked what surprised him most about humanity, he answered:

> Man! Because he sacrifices his health in order to make money. Then he sacrifices money to recuperate his health. And then he is so anxious about the future that he does not enjoy the present; the result being that he does not live in the present or the future; he lives as if he is never going to die, and then dies having never really lived.

This profound truth often rings loudest in the unexpected moments of our busiest lives—like a seemingly ordinary afternoon in my kitchen...

A Moment in Time

"Screech." My chair scraped across the hardwood floor. "That's it! You blew your last chance!" I snapped at my younger son, pushing away from the dining room table to stir the bubbling pumpkin rice on the stove. The aroma of simmering curry chicken filled the air, but my mood was anything but calm.

We had been wrestling with an algebra worksheet for over an hour—and were still on problem three. What triggered my outburst wasn't the math. It was him mimicking his older brother. The leaning back in his chair, the fluttering of half-closed eyelids, the theatrical pretense of falling asleep as I explained—again—a concept he clearly didn't want to grasp. "If he doesn't care," I muttered to myself, "why should I?"

My phone buzzed with notifications. Multiple missed calls. All from my siblings.

My stomach dropped before my mind caught up. Something must have happened. To someone in my family. Whatever it was, I wasn't ready for it.

At nearly fifty—ancient by my children's standards—I thought I'd have life figured out. But as I guided a young adult, a teenage daughter, and a teenage son through the maze of growing up, I quietly wondered if I still knew what I was doing. Or if I ever had.

Until then, I'd lived a relatively structured life—the degrees, the jobs, the steady climb. But suddenly, that path felt blurry. And what I wanted most wasn't another success story. It was *freedom*—time to breathe, space to think, and the ability to be fully present in a life that felt like mine again, while still guiding my children toward lives of their own.

Yet at that moment, I felt trapped by the same responsibilities that so many mothers do: the juggle of parenting, work, expectations, and fears. Everyone says, *"Enjoy these moments. They go by so fast."* But it didn't feel that way to me—not when the hard moments dragged on endlessly and I could barely look up long enough to truly see, let alone beam lovingly at, my children's faces.

My mind was starting to spiral when I caught myself, remembering the missed calls. My hand reached for the phone—and just as I did, it rang again.

"Mom was in a car accident," I heard my brother say. "But don't worry, she's ok."

I exhaled a breath I didn't even know I was holding.

No Time to Waste

Wake-up calls come in many forms. And sometimes, they show up right in the middle of dinner prep and math homework. That moment reminded me how little time we really have—and how much of it we spend not fully *living*.

What helped me cut through the noise—the doubts, the overwhelm, the questions—was journaling. And through that reflection, I realized something big: I wasn't writing just for myself anymore. I was writing for other mothers like me—women doing their best, feeling like it's not enough, and longing to rediscover their strength.

You might be one of those mothers. You may have tried everything—the parenting books, the expert advice, the well-intentioned articles. Most are filled with great insights. But here's what many of them miss—the fundamental truth that:

The journey to better parenting begins not with your children—but with you.

This book explores the moment everything begins to change—when you stop looking outward and start listening within.

Because when you strengthen *you*, everything else starts to shift —your energy, your influence, your ability to lead.

Using This Book

In the pages ahead, I'll share what I learned while raising three very different children—each with big dreams and strong personalities. These aren't neatly packaged lessons in chronological order. They're real, layered, and often learned side by side with my kids.

Part I lays out three core lessons that reshaped my parenting:

1. **Your children are their own force**—and that's not only okay, it's essential. You can influence but not control. Knowing when to guide and when to let go is key.

2. **Helping too much can hurt.** Studies show that many young adults struggle with resilience because they've never had space to fail.

3. **Teach independence.** "Give a man a fish, and you feed him for a day. Teach a man to fish, and you feed him for a lifetime." This isn't just a saying. It's a lifeline. Letting go of the habit of doing too much for my children is one of the hardest—and most liberating—shifts I've had to make. I had to stop giving so much and start giving them space to grow, stumble, and learn on their own.

Part II is about you.

You may need to grow, heal, or rediscover yourself before you can fully implement the lessons in Part I. This section is about clearing the internal clutter and tapping into your deeper strength and spirit.

Part III explores how to support your children as they launch—and how to reconnect with your own purpose, passions, and potential along the way.

Each chapter ends with questions to help you reflect and apply what you've learned. Take them seriously. Your answers might surprise you.

What I hope sets this book apart is that it's not just about parenting strategy. It's about the *whole person behind the parent.* Because when you strengthen the mother, you strengthen the family. Period.

This book is for you, if you've ever:

- Worried your child might not launch successfully
- Felt dismissed by your older kids who think you have nothing to offer
- Experienced conflict with a co-parent who is critical of your approach, leaving you feeling misunderstood and unsupported
- Questioned your own worth as a mother
- Battled anxiety or fear about your child's future—or your own

You are not alone. And you are not powerless.

Before we dive in, here are five core truths to keep in mind:

Don't beat yourself up. Every parent makes mistakes. The only real failure is not learning from them.

You have more power than you think. Even when it doesn't feel that way. Especially when it doesn't.

Your children can teach you, too. Listening without judgment reveals more than lecturing ever will.

Take care of you first. The oxygen mask rule isn't just for planes. It's for parenting too.

Believe that change is possible. For your kids. For your family. For *you*.

Ready? Let's begin.

Let's unlock the power within and embrace the journey back to you.

PART I
Ground Rules

You will teach them to fly, but they will not fly your flight. You will teach them to dream, but they will not dream your dream. You will teach them to live, but they will not live your life. Nevertheless, in every flight, in every life, in every dream, the print of the way you taught, will always remain.

—MOTHER TERESA

CHAPTER 1

Parent the Child You Have

Loosen the reins, so they can discover their own path

I'd just picked up my daughter from school, where she had taken her SAT, and was listening to how she left out a whole section of the test and had to do a lot of guessing. I could tell, though, as she talked to her friend on the phone, that she was bubbly with relief. She told me she was thrilled the stress was over. And as she reveled in that newfound freedom, the realization hit me: the stress she was celebrating wasn't from the test itself, but from dealing with *me*. All I could feel was intense disappointment—after thirteen weeks of a private tutor, an absurd amount of money spent—and she had to guess the answers!

Wanting What's Best

I work in technology. At the time of my daughter's SAT, most of my college friends and colleagues were living outwardly successful lives with children following in their footsteps—attending either our alma mater or receiving scholarships to Berkeley, UCLA, USC, or medical school. When I listened to their stories of academic achievement, I sometimes wondered why my children were so different.

These kids were following the paths their parents had set, going on to lucrative careers in finance, tech, medicine, or consulting. I knew I wasn't alone in believing that a good education was the surest path to success. The college admissions scandal[1] only confirmed how far some parents would go—even committing fraud—to secure their child's place at a top school.

But even in that scandal, I saw another tragedy: parents so desperate to shape their child's future that they forgot to believe in their child's own ability to create it.

As a parent, I've done everything I could—ethically and within reason—to support my kids. But an elite college wasn't in the cards for any of my children. What mattered most to them wasn't prestige or comfort. It was purpose. A calling. A sense of knowing. They each believed they were here to do something specific and meaningful, and they were determined to pursue it—on their terms.

Square Pegs and Round Holes

I tried not to compare, but sometimes I slipped. I'd mention what my friends' kids were doing. My son once responded, "Mom,

---

1 https://en.wikipedia.org/wiki/Varsity_Blues_scandal

I know so many of these kids who seem to be doing the 'right' thing. But once they get to college, they're overwhelmed, confused, depressed. I know who I am. I'm not lost. Just because I'm not doing what they're doing doesn't mean I'm doing nothing." He believed in his path, even if I couldn't yet see where it led.

He made a fair point—and I could understand where he was coming from. I still pushed. I thought he should study business or sports psychology—something useful for when he retired from the MMA and opened his own gym. I told him a degree was a smart backup.

He disagreed. "People with backup plans never go all in. I don't want that to be me."

Part of me knew he had a point. Backup plans often become the main plan. The steady job. The mortgage. The safe life.

Eventually, he agreed to attend community college. My husband and I drove him every day since he'd totaled the car we'd loaned him. He barely tried. Failed every class. It was high school all over again. I wondered if I had pushed too hard—or not hard enough. Had I given up too soon, or held on too long? The truth is, I didn't know. Parenting doesn't come with a control group.

We even tried to get him evaluated for ADHD, but he refused. He didn't want labels. He believed they put limits on people. By then he was over 18 so we couldn't force him.

With my daughter, the story was different. She wanted to go to USC. She didn't put in the work, so she didn't get in. Instead of choosing another academic path, she enrolled in a dramatic arts school. And even when we pulled privileges—like car access—she stuck to her decision.

It felt like I was trying to squeeze a square peg into a round hole. So what are parents to do? Nudge gently? Push? Or simply step aside and let them take the road they feel called to walk?

Looking back, I wish I had not put myself through all the stress. Encouraged and guided, enforced boundaries when needed—and then let go. As the saying goes: "You can lead a horse to water, but you can't make it drink."

Master of Destiny

Letting go is hard. As a parent, it feels natural to hold on. But what if that instinct to hold on is what's holding them back?

Research supports this. Studies on autonomy-supportive parenting have shown that allowing children to make their own decisions, take age-appropriate risks, and pursue their interests leads to greater psychological well-being, motivation, and long-term resilience. Children who are trusted to take the reins are more likely to become confident, self-regulating adults.

I've come to believe that it's not our job to control our children's paths. They arrive with an inner compass. And often, it's our fear and expectations that interfere with their ability to follow it.

A year later, my daughter was thriving. Top of her class. Loved by teachers. A natural leader among her peers. What changed?

She became the master of her own destiny. She chose acting, supplemented with business classes. It suited her. She was no longer boxed in by a system that didn't fit.

Our education system is outdated. It worked for the industrial age. It doesn't work for everyone now. We need systems that help young people discover their strengths and unleash their potential—not just memorize facts.

Some kids need the reins loosened. The more you pull, the more they kick. But when you let go, they run—fast, fierce, and with direction.

It is often the stubborn child, the one whom you've had the most difficulty with, that is born with an overpowering and indestructible sense of themselves. Even though their goals are not yet fully formed, and their lives may not end up being easy, they will follow their own sense of direction to discover and blaze new trails.

Consider Howard Schultz, the former CEO of Starbucks. Raised in a Brooklyn housing project by a father who never graduated high school, Schultz was expected to find a steady job and stick with it. But he had a different vision. After a trip to Italy, he was inspired to reimagine coffee shops in America—not just as places to grab a drink, but as community hubs. He left a secure position and defied expectations, taking a risk his upbringing had never prepared him for. That risk transformed how millions of people experience their daily rituals—and turned Starbucks into a global brand. Schultz didn't follow a path handed to him. He carved one out for himself.

If his parents had pushed him to stay on a "safe" path—or if he had been too afraid to diverge from their expectations—the Starbucks story might never have happened. Schultz didn't just build a company; he created a global culture by trusting his instincts over the roadmap his family might have drawn. His story reminds us that our role isn't to prescribe our children's path, but to prepare them to walk it—even when it leads somewhere we never imagined.

I thought of this again while watching *Bohemian Rhapsody*, which follows Freddie Mercury's evolution from Farrokh Bulsara, a young immigrant from Zanzibar, to one of the most electrifying performers in music history as the lead singer of *Queen*. In the film, his father repeats a mantra—"Good thoughts, good words, good deeds"—urging him toward a respectable, responsible life. Mercury, however, had no interest in fitting that mold. He wasn't defiant for the sake of rebellion; he simply knew who he was. He followed an internal rhythm, embracing what made him different—his flamboyance, his voice, even the overbite others mocked—and turned it into an unforgettable force. He didn't just break the mold. He made a new one.

That's not luck. That's courage. That's freedom. **That kind of boldness rarely blooms under pressure—it grows when someone gives you space to become yourself.**

Now that my daughter is on her path, I want her to pursue it with the same boldness. I don't regret encouraging her to stretch academically—it built grit. But the real gift was letting her go. Our relationship will recover. My voice in her ear may still serve her in the future. And real passion is tested through resistance.

Letting her take the reins gave me peace. For the first time, I felt she was truly ready to launch. And I could begin imagining my own next chapter—not as the one always leading, but as someone trotting alongside, with my own destination in sight. She's still figuring it out, of course—just like most of us. But she's motivated now in a way she never was when I was steering. And that shift alone tells me we're heading in the right direction.

The poet, Khalil Gibran wrote:

> Your children are not your children. They are the sons and daughters of Life's longing for itself. They came through you but not from you, and though they are with you, they belong not to you.[2]

So, what choice do we have but to let them be free?

I came across this Facebook post[3] that reminds people to let their children be free to become whoever they are meant to be:

It reminded me of the truth I needed to hear—and maybe the one you do, too.

> Dear Parents
>
> The exams of your children are to start soon. I know you are all really anxious for your child to do well.
>
> But, please do remember, amongst the students who will be sitting for the exams there is an artist, who doesn't need to understand Math... There is

---

2 *The Prophet* by Khalil Gibran (Macmillan, 2016)
3 https://www.businessinsider.com/principal-note-to-parents-testing-2017-11

an entrepreneur, who doesn't care about History or English literature... There is a musician, whose Chemistry marks won't matter... There's an athlete... whose physical fitness is more important than Physics... If your child does get top marks, that's great! But if he or she doesn't... please don't take away their self-confidence and dignity from them. Tell them it's OK, it's just an exam! They are cut out for much bigger things in life. Tell them, no matter what they score... you love them and will not judge them.

Please do this, and when you do... watch your children conquer the world. One exam or a low mark won't take away... their dreams and talent. And please, do not think that doctors and engineers... are the only happy people in the world.

With warm Regards

Power to Let Them Lead

In a perfect world—one without distractions, temptations, or fears—you might be willing to relinquish control and let your children find their own way. However, to counteract the negative pressure of social media, peers, and the financial necessities of the real world, we push, we worry, we plan. While some kids comply and even flourish; others—the strong-willed, the independent, the ones with a different fire—they resist. And what if that resistance isn't defiance at all? What if it's destiny, and our true power lies in recognizing and nurturing it?

Your child is not here to replicate your life. They are here to create their own.

Letting go doesn't mean you give up or stop caring. It comes after you've tried: setting structure, creating opportunities, offering support, and holding expectations. It's what happens when you recognize that the next step has to come from them—and that sometimes, *not* forcing is the bravest choice you can make.

Some children thrive under pressure; others crumble. Some need to be pushed; others need to feel trusted. Studies show that when children feel respected and involved in decision-making, they develop higher levels of intrinsic motivation and emotional resilience. Letting go doesn't mean absence—it means showing up differently. Knowing that difference is part of our growth as parents.

Letting go doesn't mean disappearing. It means staying present, but shifting roles—from director to coach, from controller to companion.

See your child for who they are, not who you want them to be. You have released something extraordinary into the world. Guide them—but let their own force lead the way.

QUESTIONS TO JOURNAL

- Do you give your child enough freedom to explore their own interests and passions? Or do you restrict them to activities that will look good on a college application?

- Do you compare your child to yourself, friends, or relatives? Could your well-meaning push for them to reach their potential be interpreted as they are "not good enough" as they are?

- Think of three very successful people. Imagine them as teenagers with parents pressuring them towards a different path. What would that feel like for them? How might they have responded?

- Envision your child taking the reins of their own life. Does that make you nervous? Scared? What else does it bring up?

> We worry about what a child will become tomorrow, yet we forget that he is someone today.
>
> —Stacia Tauscher

CHAPTER 2

Let Them Struggle, Let Them Grow

If you knock down every hurdle, they'll never learn to jump

It was summer, and we were visiting my sister in the Cayman Islands. The sound of waves crashed softly outside, children's laughter danced through the patio doors, and the aroma of jerk chicken from the beach bar next door teased my senses. But instead of enjoying the warm beach and carefree vacation, I was indoors, helping my daughter slog through a practice SAT test. The plan was simple: one test in the morning, then the beach all afternoon. But she slept in, dawdled through breakfast, and didn't sit down until 2 p.m.

Twenty minutes in, I was just beginning to feel relief that we might get through it when she dropped her pencil. "Mom, I have a headache. I can't do this anymore." I glanced toward my sister, silently asking how hard I should push. The beach was calling, but so was my belief in follow-through.

We never made it to the beach that day. But looking back, that wasn't the real loss. The deeper lesson was about discernment—knowing when to push, and when to pause. I hadn't mastered it yet. But this moment planted the seed.

Black and White

One lesson I wish I had learned earlier—that **discipline is most effective when it's clear and unwavering.** But my instinct, born from a desire to understand and protect, often led me into the murky 'grey' areas.

Because I remember what it's like to be a child, I instinctively empathize. I want to explain consequences, give context, offer a path to understanding. But often, those explanations turn into negotiations. And sometimes—too often—I soften the punishment. What my children learn isn't about right and wrong; they learn that arguing might work. They don't see nuance—they see openings. And they learn to exploit them.

I've never believed in "because I said so" approach of earlier generations. I value fairness, communication, and nuance. But for that, I've paid a price. It might have been easier if I couldn't see both sides, if my words carried the final authority, if I could simply draw the line and walk away.

Some parents insist that kids need to be forced to follow through. That if you make them repeat something often enough—say, finishing homework or practicing piano—they'll eventually adopt it as their own. And yes, sometimes it works. I've seen parents hold the line with remarkable discipline—and sometimes, the payoff is visible. A neighbor's husband makes their son rewrite his essays until they meet his standard. The son used to cry. Now he beams when his test scores come back—100% across the board.

Or the soccer dad who pressured his son to keep playing, even when he resisted. Eventually, with practice and praise, the child not only loved the game—he made the national team.

Sometimes the pressure comes from the culture itself. Growing up in Jamaica, we didn't have endless options. You became a doctor, lawyer, or engineer/programmer. All four of us siblings did. The structure of our world propelled us. In contrast, American kids today swim in choices. If their heart isn't in academics, forcing them through it feels like dragging water uphill.

Of course, not all stories of parental pressure end in rebellion. Some children achieve greatness precisely because of a parent's relentless drive—though often with complicated emotional consequences. Take Andre Agassi, who became a tennis legend but later revealed in his autobiography *Open* that he hated the sport. His father forced him to hit thousands of balls a day, designing a machine nicknamed "The Dragon" to keep him training at a brutal pace. While Agassi reached the pinnacle of professional success, he struggled with identity, depression, and resentment along the way.

In contrast, consider Venus and Serena Williams. Their father, Richard Williams, also imposed a highly structured plan for their tennis careers from a young age. But unlike Agassi, both sisters embraced the sport and thrived—not just athletically, but emotionally and professionally. They credit their success to both their father's vision and the passion they developed for the game.

These examples show that forcing can yield results—but sometimes at a cost. When a child's internal compass aligns with the external pressure, it may work. But when it doesn't, the price might be motivation, mental health, or even the parent-child bond. It's not just *what* we push our children toward—it's *why* and *how* we do it that determines whether we help or hinder their future.

Witnessing these divergent paths—and reflecting on my own struggles—forced me to fundamentally reconsider my approach: what I was doing, and what I might be missing. I've tried to hold firm—especially when I know my child's heart is still in it. If my younger son wants to skip basketball because the coach is tough, but I know he loves the game, I make him go. That kind of resistance feels like discomfort, not misalignment. And sometimes, pushing through it builds resilience.

But when the resistance runs deeper—when it's not just mood or motivation, but something internal pushing back—the outcome shifts. I once insisted my daughter finish an SAT practice test before she could leave the table. She ended up with a real headache—and a hospital visit. Afterward, I gave her a choice: SAT tutor or no more weekend concerts. She chose the tutor but barely engaged. The drive wasn't hers. And without that, nothing stuck.

So where's the line?

Too much force can create resentment or helplessness, especially when the goal doesn't resonate with the child. On the other hand, too little structure—what's often called permissive parenting—leaves them unmoored. Children aren't mini-adults. Their brains are still developing. They need limits, guidance, and accountability. A teenager with total freedom might skip school or worse—and the consequences may not appear until the damage is harder to undo.

Performing Somersaults

The battle between letting go and holding on isn't reserved for grand life decisions; it unfolds daily, demanding we perform mental somersaults in the smallest moments of parenting. Most of the parents I know aren't strictly authoritarian or permissive. We fall somewhere in the middle—what psychologists call authoritative[4]: high expectations paired with emotional warmth. And yet, even those of us with the best intentions falter in execution.

We aim for structure, but don't always enforce it. We set rules, but don't follow through on consequences. So, we end up in familiar scenes, like Sunday night homework emergencies.

I used to finish my homework on Friday. So it drove me crazy when my child would call to me at 9 p.m. on Sunday needing help. I'd say, "It's late. You'll have to figure it out yourself." And I meant it. Until they said, "If I fail, it's your fault."

---

4 https://www.verywellfamily.com/ways-to-become-a-more-authoritative-parent-4136329

That statement—so wrong it shouldn't merit a response—sucked me in every time. And despite being exhausted, I'd sit down and help them finish.

The problem is we want them to do well in school more than they want it themselves. So, we are the ones performing somersaults and turning ourselves inside out in pursuit of excellent grades. **We absorb their stress because we're afraid of what might happen if we don't.** For us, good grades lead to good schools, which leads to good jobs and a comfortable living. Because they haven't yet discovered this for themselves, it feels as if the burden of their academic success falls on us.

We're tired. So instead of holding the line, we cross it ourselves—and do the work for them. We take on our children's tasks as if they were our own because we are anxious and fearful of how significant, drastic, and irreversible the consequences would be if they don't get them done. **But when we carry their burden, they never learn to lift it themselves.**

Experts Recommend

There's no perfect parenting formula. But these strategies can help:

> **Control the environment, not just behavior.** Don't expect your child to self-regulate if their phone, Xbox or TikTok is still buzzing. As the parent providing the device, you have the right and responsibility to set limits accordingly.

Praise effort, not just results. Intrinsic motivation grows when kids feel proud of what they've accomplished on their own.

Build habits. Create a consistent time and place for homework—daily, not just when there's a crisis.

Be clear. Post the rules. "You may watch TV for one hour, after the homework is complete and checked."

Use logical consequences. If they make a mess, they clean it up—plus sweep the entire room. No arbitrary punishments.

Stay Consistent. Every choice should have a predictable outcome: Choice A = Outcome A, Choice B = Outcome B, as if you were writing a computer program.

Still struggling? Let natural consequences step in—as long as they're safe, timely, and clearly tied to the child's actions.

Don't become the parent Julie Lythcott-Haims describes in *How to Raise an Adult*—the one who shadows their kids into college, managing every bump in the road. Instead, detach from outcomes. **Guide. Don't rescue.**

That's how they grow. That's how you breathe.

Natural Consequences

The more I've practiced letting my children face the natural outcomes of their choices, the better I've become at it. When my daughter was preparing to leave for college, I warned her not to overpack. She didn't listen. At the airport, the luggage was overweight, and the airline charged a $75 fee. I gave her a lecture—but still paid the fine.

She didn't learn much from that. So, the next time, I didn't pay. I told her to speak with the airline staff and get a plastic bag to put her excess stuff. On her third flight, I let her manage the situation entirely. She negotiated with the clerk, made it through security, and was in the lounge by the time I called her back. She figured it out—and probably gained more confidence from that than anything I could have taught her directly.

Later trips? I didn't hear about them. She'd learned that her actions had consequences—and that she could handle them.

With my younger son, I've learned to let natural consequences do the work, too. If he skips showers after basketball practice and ends up embarrassed by the way he smells, he learns. No lectures required. When he tries to shift the blame—"You should have made me"—I remind him: you're responsible now. That's how growth begins.

What changed wasn't just their behavior—it was mine. I stopped rushing in. And that pause created the space they needed to rise.

Owning Their Goals

When kids choose a goal that truly matters to them, it opens the door for growth. I used to own their ambitions for them—reminding, pushing, planning. But when my younger son wanted to attend a respected Catholic school, I stepped back. I told him the GPA and test scores required. I helped him understand the benchmarks. But the effort had to be his.

He didn't get in—his decision came too late to turn around his grades. But he crushed the high school placement test and walked away with two life-changing lessons: that focused effort pays off, and that success is ultimately in his hands.

Even though the consequences of your child's choices and actions may not be what you or they hoped for, they may be just what your child needs.

Take a Breath and a Break

Letting go of outcomes doesn't mean giving up. It means giving your child room to grow—and giving yourself the relief of not carrying their every burden.

We live in a messy world. Parenting doesn't come with perfect conditions. Our kids are shaped by their peers, their screens, and a society that gives them power before they're ready. We make mistakes. So do they.

But when we stop shielding them from their own consequences, we finally make space for change. For them—and for us.

As Doris Day sang, "*Que sera, sera—whatever will be, will be.*" It's not surrender. It's wisdom.

Power to Let Them Fail

Children will test boundaries. That's what they do. Your job is to stand firm and clear. Let your yes mean yes, and your no mean no. If they sense your rules are malleable, they'll push. But if your follow-through is consistent, they'll learn where the lines are—and start walking within them.

We hate watching our children struggle. But the only way they'll develop resilience is to feel failure, manage it, and rise. Don't rob them of that. Let them fail. Let them get back up. And let them become stronger than even you believed possible.

QUESTIONS TO JOURNAL

- What parenting style are you—authoritarian (high demands, low responsiveness), permissive (low demands, high responsiveness), or authoritative (high demands, high responsiveness)? What impact is this having on your child—and on you?
- Can your child predict the logical consequence of breaking a rule? Why or why not?
- Think of a time you saved your child from a consequence. Did it help them learn—or repeat the mistake?
- Is the natural consequence of their action safe, timely, and clearly connected? If so, can you let it happen, even if it's hard to watch?

Parents who are afraid to put their foot down usually have children who step on their toes.

—Chinese proverb

CHAPTER 3

Raising Doers, Not Dependents

Teach Them to Fish—and Then Step Away from the Shore

For years, every time I asked my husband to put away the dishes or help out in the kitchen, his reply was always the same: "Don't ask me—teach your kids." It irritated me to no end. But deep down, I knew he wasn't wrong.

Our children should have been expected to pitch in. And not just expected—trained. I remember my husband visiting his teammate's family in Peru and coming back impressed: even the toddler helped set the table and clean up. It wasn't a chore—it was just what they did. "We have to teach them how to fish," he said. And I bristled. I wanted to shout, "You think I haven't tried? They don't listen! *They're just like you!*"

But over time, I realized something. I hadn't fully claimed my power. When I finally stood firm—assigning each of our three kids a dish for Christmas dinner and insisting they follow through—something shifted. My husband followed suit, suddenly pitching in without being asked. And I saw it clearly: this is what he'd been waiting for all along—not speeches, but leadership.

Fishing Lessons

My husband was right: parenting isn't about handing over fish—it's about patiently teaching your child to hold the rod, cast the line, and eventually reel in on their own. That Christmas dinner was a turning point. I wasn't doing the task for them or softening my expectations—I was leading. And to my surprise, everyone followed.

For a long time, though, I believed some kids were just naturally more helpful. I'd ask parents of responsible children what they did, and they'd often say, "She's just like her mom," or "He's always been that way." I wondered if helpfulness was simply inherited—something you were either born with or not.

But personality is not destiny. Sure, kids come with their own traits. But they also learn from what we do—or don't do. If we blame temperament, we minimize the real, powerful influence of nurture. Our children aren't blank slates, but they're certainly unfinished stories.

In my professional life, I manage teams. I delegate, coach, motivate. I don't step in every time someone falters. I guide. I hold them accountable. But when it comes to parenting, it often felt harder. A parenting adviser we consulted about helping our older son launch once told my husband—himself a sports coach—"Motivational speeches won't work on your son. You need a stronger approach. A firmer hand and a clearer plan"

That stuck with me.

What Doesn't Work Well

My journey to raising independent 'doers' wasn't without significant detours. Before I discovered what truly worked, I, like many parents, stumbled into plenty of common traps:

- **Competitions and rewards** can spark short-term action, but they don't build long-term habits. Kids catch on to manipulation fast.
- **Forced family fun**—like blasting music while doing chores—might charm one child and annoy another.
- **Nagging** is the default mode of many frustrated parents—and nearly always a waste of breath.

FREE: The Framework

Over time, I began to find a better way. One rooted in values and habits, not bribes or blowups. I call it **FREE**, because when your children no longer rely on you, *you* are finally *free* too:

Foster: Encourage a spirit of giving and teamwork, both in the home and in the world.

Routine: Make doing chores and helping around the house part of their routine, not a special request.

Earn: Instead of giving freely, let them work for what they want—it teaches value.

Expect more: Raise the bar steadily and believe they can reach it.

Each piece of this framework moves them toward independence—and lifts a burden off your shoulders. Let me show you how each one played out in our home, starting with the simple but powerful act of giving.

Foster

Every year, our family volunteers at a long-standing charity event in Richmond, started over seventy years ago by a friend's grandfather. We hand out books, toys, and soccer balls to hundreds of underprivileged children. My daughter lights up as she interacts with the families, while my younger son, quieter but observant, seems to absorb the significance of each small act of generosity on the lives of these children and their families.

It's a powerful reminder that we don't need more time or money to give back—we just need the willingness to show up. That single afternoon brings more perspective than a hundred lectures ever could. But once a year wasn't enough. I realized that volunteering needed to be a family affair, woven into the fabric of our lives and not just reserved for special occasions. So we started smaller, closer to home—spending time with grandparents who appreciated the company, helping a friend organize her garage, or bringing snacks to sports games. I saw how even these simple acts created a shift. My children began to see themselves as capable of helping, not just needing help. That shift in identity is subtle but powerful. Contribution breeds confidence.

Marc Benioff, CEO of Salesforce, came to a similar realization after spending time with Buddhist monks in India. Inspired, he implemented a company culture where new employees begin their first day of work volunteering in schools, shelters, or hospitals. The impact? Profound. His employees gain empathy, perspective, and a commitment to community that follows them back into the workplace.

Kids raised in an environment where giving is the norm—not the exception—learn to value contribution over consumption. And when children see the real needs of others, they often find a deeper reason to become capable and self-reliant.

Routine

Creating a routine of household responsibilities is critical— especially while kids are still young. If helping is built into the rhythm of their lives early on, it becomes second nature. By the time schoolwork and activities ramp up, they'll already have the muscle memory for pitching in.

I remember the first time I flossed my teeth properly. It took nearly an hour, and I called a friend who's an orthodontist to complain. But because I stuck with it, flossing now takes me five minutes. The same principle applies to chores. Once expectations are clear and practiced regularly, what once felt like a battle becomes simply a habit.

But getting there wasn't easy. At first, routines felt like a war of wills. I'd remind them, they'd forget. I'd threaten, they'd stall.

Every day felt like starting from scratch. The breakthrough didn't come from nagging—it came from clarity and consistency. I stopped asking. I wrote down the expectations and put them where everyone could see. And I followed through.

With my younger son, we finally found a system that works: a magnetic chore board on the fridge. When he completes his tasks—unloading the dishwasher, emptying garbage cans—he earns extra minutes on his device or a couple of dollars added to the stash I keep in my purse. I think part of him genuinely recognizes that doing his share isn't just fair—it's good for him.

There's pride in routine. When kids see themselves as contributors, they show up differently. Not because we told them to—but because they've started telling themselves: *I've got this.*

Earn

Esther Wojcicki, mother of three extraordinarily accomplished daughters—including the prior CEOs of YouTube and 23andMe—once shared her parenting philosophy in an acronym: TRICK—Trust, Respect, Independence, Collaboration, and Kindness. One moment that caught my attention was her story of dropping her grandkids off at Target with a list of school supplies and letting them handle the task themselves. She trusted them. And they rose to meet that trust.

She also believed in making kids work for what they wanted. "I didn't give them anything," she told Forbes. "Even when they were little—they had to earn it."[5]

---

5 https://www.forbes.com/sites/cartercoudriet/2019/06/18/esther-wojcicki-parenting-susan-anne-janet-women-summit/#72f14b3c1541

This approach made sense to me. I've known many parents who didn't grow up with much and now feel compelled to give their kids everything they never had. Others, including me, gave freely simply because we could—and because it felt good. At birthdays and Christmas, within reason, their wish was my command. I wanted to see them excited, not disappointed.

But over the years, I learned a few things. One: if you give a person an inch, they take a mile. I remember telling my daughter that she never seemed satisfied—that if I offered her a trip to London and Paris, she'd ask to see Rome. I lay in the bed that I made but realized I needed to remake it.

The cost of giving had become unsustainable—not just financially, but emotionally. So, we did a reset. One Christmas, the kids helped prepare the meal. The gifts were thoughtful but modest. And to my surprise, the holiday was better than ever. Their initial disappointment in the gifts faded quickly. What lasted was the pride of contribution, the joy of being part of something—a wonderful Christmas dinner and an ongoing family tradition.

And here's what else I learned: no matter how much effort you put in to please them, at some point your kids will be disappointed. Or worse, they'll accuse you of breaking a promise you don't even remember making. If you're not careful, they'll wrap you around their finger with guilt or manipulation. But when you let them earn what they want, they gain something far more valuable: self-respect, resourcefulness, and perspective.

I saw this firsthand with my older son. During the pandemic, when our cleaning lady couldn't come, he took responsibility for the kids' bathroom. He didn't just wipe things down—he scrubbed every surface until it sparkled. Then something incredible happened: he became its guardian. He made sure his siblings didn't mess it up and took pride in keeping it clean. For the first time, I saw him own a task from beginning to end. It changed how he viewed work—and how I viewed his capability.

Each of these moments unlocks a piece of your child's independence. They begin to shape not just what they do, but who they believe they are. And with every small act of ownership, you get to step back a little more—out of the spotlight, but never out of their corner.

Expect More

Psychologists recommend setting expectations that are high but also reasonable. If you expect too much too soon, kids may feel like they're constantly falling short. But if you expect too little, they settle for less and underestimate their potential. It's a delicate balance—one that evolves over time.

I had high expectations for my kids. I expected good grades, musical talent, athletic achievement. I envisioned them excelling like my husband and I once did. But reality didn't match the vision. None of my children fit that mold exactly. My daughter showed early promise in music, but her interests shifted. My younger son was asked by his piano teacher to drop the class—she said he just wasn't ready to learn. And though my children all had natural gifts, academic excellence didn't come easily for any of them.

With my younger son, I may have inadvertently lowered expectations too much. Managing his daily homework and basketball practice felt like a major win, and I didn't pile on more tasks, even small ones. I saw how he struggled with multi-step instructions and took longer to grasp routines; challenges often associated with ADHD. I convinced myself that his struggles were more about nature than nurture. But if I was honest, I also saw my own fixed mindset creeping in: a belief that his abilities were inherently limited, making me fear that pushing him too hard would only lead to frustration. In contrast, a friend's daughter with ADHD was given just one new expectation at a time—like organizing her backpack each evening. By the end of the semester, she was handling her entire morning routine solo. It reminded me that high expectations don't need to be big. They just need to be consistent. It wasn't about setting the bar high all at once—but lifting it just enough to invite a stretch.

That shift—away from a fixed mindset and toward a growth mindset—changed everything.

Now, I try to expect gradual, steady growth. I watch for progress, not perfection. Even when my son pleads for help with a task he just demonstrated he can do, I resist the urge to step in. I step back. I give him space to figure it out on his own. Because I know that when I do, he eventually does. And with every small success, his confidence grows.

Praising his effort—not just the outcome—helps, too. When he knows I see how hard he's trying, he's more willing to keep going. Over time, I've come to believe that expecting more is not about pushing our kids to reach unrealistic goals—**it's about** trusting that with support, belief, and consistent effort, they can reach further than we imagined.

Growth or Fixed

Psychologist Carol Dweck, who developed the concept of the growth mindset, describes two distinct belief systems about learning and ability[6]:

> **Fixed mindset:** "In a fixed mindset, people believe their basic qualities, like their intelligence or talent, are simply fixed traits. They spend their time documenting their intelligence or talent instead of developing them. They also believe that talent alone creates success—without effort."
>
> **Growth mindset:** "In a growth mindset, people believe that their most basic abilities can be developed through dedication and hard work—brains and talent are just the starting point. This view creates a love of learning and a resilience that is essential for great accomplishment."

A fixed mindset can be paralyzing. I know, because I've lived it. As a child, I was often praised for being "smart." But instead of building confidence, it created pressure. I became cautious, avoiding situations where I might not know the answer—afraid that falling short would mean I wasn't as smart as everyone thought. If a conversation felt like a quiz, I would shrink back rather than risk getting it wrong.

---

6 Mindset: The New Psychology of Success by Carol Dweck (Robinson, 2015)

My older son, who is bright and quick-witted, may be plagued with a similar limiting belief. I remember when he was about eight or nine, he impressed our relatives with an impromptu eulogy of his cousin's goldfish, which was both brilliant and amusing. At family gatherings, he'd steal the spotlight with spontaneous and hilarious impersonations. Everyone believed he was destined for greatness. We praised his intelligence, his humor, his charm—constantly. But in hindsight, we may have praised the wrong things.

At fifteen, he won a gold medal in a jiu-jitsu tournament and was sponsored by Ralph Gracie. It seemed like the beginning of his dream to become a UFC champion. But the following year, after losing a wrestling match, he never competed again. It was as if failure had confirmed a hidden fear—that maybe he wasn't as good as people believed. And instead of pushing through, he retreated.

Research supports this pattern. **When children are praised primarily for their talent or intelligence, they can become more fragile—not more resilient.** The moment they face failure, they interpret it not as a challenge to overcome, but as a threat to their identity. They give up or avoid trying altogether.

In contrast, children with a growth mindset see failure as part of the process. They accept feedback, seek out ways to improve, and keep going when things get tough. I've seen this in some of the people I've managed professionally. They crave feedback—not because they're insecure, but because they want to grow. They advance quickly, not necessarily because they're more talented, but because they're more open to learning.

This is the mindset I'm working to cultivate in my children—and in myself. I remind them that talent is just the starting point, not the finish line. I praise effort, persistence, and progress. And when I feel the urge to protect them from failure, I ask myself: Am I helping them? Or am I holding them back?

Because the truth is, a child who believes they can improve—with effort, patience, and time—can accomplish far more than one who believes success depends on being naturally gifted. Even the most talented among us, like Kobe Bryant, trained as if they had none. **That mindset, more than any natural gift, is what carries people to greatness.**

Power to Trade Control for Trust

It often feels easier to just do things yourself—especially when you know the garbage will be done properly, the dishwasher loaded more efficiently, or the dinner ready on time. And in the short term, it is easier. But in the long run, **doing everything yourself keeps the burden on your shoulders and robs your children of the very experiences they need to grow.**

The same is true emotionally. It's easier to offer comfort than to enforce structure. Easier to swoop in and fix the problem than to let them wrestle with the discomfort of figuring it out. But if we're always rescuing them, we deny them the opportunity to build resilience, confidence, and independence.

That's why the goal isn't perfection—it's progress. One step at a time, we hand over the reins. One responsibility at a time, we stop doing and start coaching. One expectation at a time, we raise the bar just high enough for them to stretch.

There's a teaching principle that captures this perfectly[7]: *Show me, help me, let me.* The problem is, many of us get stuck in the "help me" phase, never moving on to "let me." We justify it because we love them, or because they seem too fragile, or because it's faster. But holding on too long stunts their growth and drains us in the process.

Moms, you have the power to promote self-reliance and independence. You do this by creating a culture that values contribution (**Foster**), builds habits of responsibility (**Routine**), emphasizes effort and ownership (**Earn**), and trusts your child to grow beyond today's limitations (**Expect More**).

When your child no longer depends on you for everything, it's not a loss. It's a gift—for them, and for you. Because that's when they truly begin to soar. And you? You get to walk beside them, proud, lighter, and finally free. That's the real payoff—not just their independence, but your own transformation too.

QUESTIONS TO JOURNAL

- In what ways does a child who volunteers appear different from a child who doesn't? Do you notice a difference in their values, how they treat others, or their level of confidence in themselves?

---

[7] *Action Strategies for Deepening Comprehension* by Jeffrey D. Wilhelm (Scholastic Professional Books, 2002)

- When a child performs regular chores at home, how does the rest of the family react when the task goes undone? What does that teach your child about responsibility, not just personally but to everyone else around?

- When you give your child things that they want but don't need, does it make them more generous in return—or more expectant? How can you begin to turn this around and have your child earn what they want instead?

- When you do things for your child that they can do for themselves, do you consider this helping—or hindering?

- Imagine two children with similar abilities: One child's mother sits next to them each day while doing homework; the other's parent checks in periodically when the child needs help or to make sure it is complete. Which child do you think has more confidence and self-reliance? Which mother feels calmer, more in control, and more intentional in how she supports her child's growth?

> Tell me, and I forget.
> Teach me, and I remember.
> Involve me, and I learn.
>
> —Benjamin Franklin

PART II
Self-transformation

When we change, the world changes. The key to all change is in our inner transformation—a change of our hearts and minds. This is human revolution. We all have the power to change. When we realize this truth, we can bring forth that power anywhere, anytime, and in any situation.

—DAISAKU IKEDA[8]

---

8 https://www.daisakuikeda.org/sub/resources/works/essays/buddhist-essays/what-is-human-revolution.html

CHAPTER 4

Mind Games

*Control Your Mind Before
It Takes Control of You*

One day, I made a mistake. I told my older son, "Go cut your hair. I don't like the clothes you're wearing—they're dirty and barely fit. You look like someone who's lost on the streets of Jamaica." There's no justifying what I said. And at the time, I didn't think it was a big deal. But the truth is, it wasn't just about hygiene or appearance. What I saw—messy hair, clothes that didn't quite fit—tapped into something deeper: my fear. Not of how he looked, but of what it might mean. I worried he was slipping away from the path we had hoped for him. In that moment, those outward signs felt symbolic, stirring up all the love and concern I had for his future—and the fear that he might lose sight of his own potential.

When I said those words, he laughed, danced around with his siblings, and pretended to be the "crazy man" I had described. But then he stopped. He looked at me—seriously, steadily, with those light brown eyes that always seemed to see more than I wanted to show—and said, "Mom, how can you say this? Why are you putting me down? Shouldn't you be building me up? I can see in your eyes that you're lost. Only when you find yourself can you be the person I can follow. Go find yourself. Go talk to God or something."

His words were a revelation, piercing through my defenses. They didn't just hit; they embedded themselves deep within my mind, a persistent echo that amplified during the long, sleepless nights when my own anxieties about the future spiraled beyond my control.

Lost in Anxiety

It wasn't the first time my son had challenged me like that. Even with all the love, time, and energy my husband and I had poured into our children—the after-school activities, the tutoring, the encouragement, the travel—our son still questioned whether we were worth following. I saw it as entitlement, because sometimes it was. But separate from that, I also had to face a harder truth: I was *lost*.

Not physically. Mentally. Emotionally. Spiritually.

I didn't know when exactly I had unraveled, but I knew I had. And I needed to find my way back.

As a child, I was a bit of a hypochondriac. It didn't help that my parents, both doctors, regularly discussed their patients' ailments over dinner. The smallest symptom would grow in my mind until it felt life-threatening. A sniffle became the flu. A heart flutter meant I was dying. People often say that listening to your heartbeat can help calm anxiety—but for me, it made things worse. I would focus so hard on the rhythm that I convinced myself it was too fast, too erratic or skipping. My chest pounded, my breath quickened, and I would panic, running to my mother terrified that something was terribly wrong.

Even into adulthood, anxiety stayed with me. Traveling alone with the kids? Cue the panic. Medicine wouldn't help. Sleep wouldn't come. My mind had become more powerful than my body.

The breaking point came a few years ago, right before a business trip to Europe. My aunt and uncle had passed away weeks apart. I was grieving, exhausted, and allergy-congested. I became convinced I wouldn't be able to breathe on the plane. The more I fixated on it, the worse the feeling got. A lump formed in my throat, and I was sure I'd spiral into a full-blown anxiety attack midair. I wanted to cancel the trip—but I knew it wouldn't be good for my career.

The flight was a nightmare. I was up constantly, panicked, pacing to the bathroom while the man next to me looked increasingly alarmed. Paris had just experienced a terrorist attack, so everyone was on edge. But the true threat at this moment wasn't me. It wasn't in the cabin. **My real enemy was inside my own head.**

For months afterward, I couldn't sleep. I'd bolt awake in the middle of the night, gripped by fear. I went to doctors, allergy specialists, ENT appointments. I read blogs, spoke to friends, and devoured books on anxiety. But nothing worked.

Until one night, desperate for relief, I wandered the hallway alone. I noticed the light glowing under my son's door—he was still awake. I paused, then gently knocked.

Finding Faith

I didn't expect much. I just needed to distract myself from my thoughts. But he looked at me calmly, met my distress with unwavering presence, and said, "Stay positive. Trust. Believe in God. You *will* get better."

Why, after months of doctors and desperate searching, did his simple words break through? Perhaps it was the sheer exhaustion, the utter surrender to a moment of grace. Or maybe it was the purity of a younger person's unwavering belief, untainted by the cynicism that often comes with age.

It wasn't just what he said. It was how he said it. With total certainty. No hesitation. No fear. He believed it completely—**and after a while I began to believe it too.**

That moment began my healing.

Each night, I came back to his room. Each time, he said the same words. And slowly, they started to take root. I stopped fixating on my symptoms and began turning my attention to something deeper—something eternal and grounding.

I focused on God.

Not as a distant deity, but as an unshakable force within me. I started small: just five minutes of quiet prayer each morning, repeating simple affirmations of trust—trust in God, trust in my own inner resilience, and trust that healing was possible. I listened to uplifting music that filled me with peace. I looked for moments of grace throughout my day—my children's laughter, birds chirping, a gorgeous sunset—and consciously connected them to that feeling of unwavering presence. And eventually, the joy came back. My body followed my mind into healing.

This profound shift illuminated a truth I'd always known intellectually but now experienced viscerally: the incredible power of the mind over the body. It's a phenomenon seen in countless lives; I'm sure you've seen it, too—friends or family members so overwhelmed by stress at work or in relationships that they've ended up in the ER. Maybe you've watched someone get consumed by anxiety over something they couldn't control, then seek medication to quiet the chaos. The mind can create illness—but it can also be a source of profound healing.

That's the miracle of belief. Medical studies on the placebo effect show us that under the right conditions, even a sugar pill can lead to real healing. Why? **Because when the brain believes healing is possible, the body often follows.**

When we learn to call on our internal reserves—our higher self, intuition, faith, or whatever name you give it—we begin to quiet the noise and return to truth. That is the doorway to health, peace, and power.

And yet, in this modern life, many of us have lost our way. We are overwhelmed by broken relationships, worried about our children, drowning in work stress, and cut off from our own stillness. Society shouts at us from every direction about who we're supposed to be. Our heads are filled with advice, opinions, fear. But what we're missing—what we're aching for—is an anchor. The rock. An unshakable belief in ourselves.

When everything around you is turbulent, stop. Close your eyes. Take a breath. Find the stillness within. That is where the answers live—not outside, but inside. Not in the noise, but in the quiet knowing of your own truth.

Children as Teachers

Each time I worried about my son's appearance, I was focusing on the surface, on the external picture of what I thought 'success' or 'well-being' should look like. But true growth, as he taught me, isn't just what you see on the surface or the external trappings of success. It's the discipline and control over your mind and the profound insights you gain about life.

Growth and learning in the parent-child relationship isn't just one way. If you keep an open heart and mind, you'll find that **you have as much to learn from your children as you have to teach them.** My son taught me a life-changing lesson on the incredible power of belief. We can use it to our advantage or disadvantage by achieving great things or brainwashing ourselves into believing the worst.

Despite my concerns about my son's future, I know there is something to be said about his unwavering self-belief and what he believes God has destined for him to become. He is following his own path, his own truth, and his own way, wherever it may lead.

The Impact on Our Kids

Anxiety is contagious. You might think you're shielding your kids from it, but they feel it anyway. I know a mother who checks her son's grades online twice a day. She panics at any dip below an A. She tells him to relax before tests—but her eyes, her energy, her urgency say the opposite.

Children don't follow what we say. They absorb what we feel.

It starts with a single thought: "If my child doesn't study, he'll fail the test. If he fails, he won't get into a good college. He won't have a good life. He'll live in our basement forever." The chain reaction begins, creating tension in the home.

Eventually, that fear transfers. Your child starts to believe: "My mom doesn't think I can do this." They get anxious. They withdraw. Or they rebel. The very outcome you fear becomes the reality you help create.

This is why we must control our minds—not just for ourselves, but for our children.

As humans, we tend to home in on negative possibilities and catastrophic outcomes. Anxiety takes over and turns minor concerns into imagined disasters. You may have valid reasons to worry—about your health, your children, or the state of the world—but when those thoughts consume your ability to rest, reflect, or feel joy, they become destructive. The key is to recognize when your mind is snowballing and stop it before it turns into an avalanche.

As parents, we have to train ourselves to recognize the current pulling us under—and step out of it. Our mental resilience isn't just for our own peace; it's the foundation our children stand on.

When we focus on what's lacking—what isn't right, what might go wrong—we create blockages. We resist the flow of abundance, possibility, and connection. But when we shift our minds toward gratitude, when we focus on what we have and meet our children with calm instead of anxiety, something changes. Our energy changes. And that energy gives our children permission to step into their own joy and power.

Tools for Mental Wellbeing

Psychologists and spiritual teachers alike recommend tools to calm and re-center the mind:

Physical: Walking, running, dancing, yoga

Mental & Spiritual: Meditation, mindfulness, prayer, music, gratitude practices

Nature & Connection: Being outdoors, lying in the sun, spending time with animals

Giving: Helping others, spending meaningful time with family and the community

If you're deep in the grip of anxiety, however, even these practices can feel out of reach. So here are a few gentle ways to begin, especially when you're in the thick of it:

1. Breathe anyway.
Slow, deep breaths. In for four counts, out for six. It might seem small or ineffective in the moment, but slowing your breath sends a signal to your nervous system that you're safe. It's a simple place to begin, and sometimes that's enough to break the cycle.

2. Find your ground.
When my mind started racing, I would touch something physical—the bathroom countertop, the floor under my feet, a cup of tea. Sometimes I would lean over the steam of a boiling hot mug and just breathe it in, letting it calm me from the inside out. Grounding yourself in the present moment interrupts the fear loop.

3. Speak gently to yourself.
I would repeat simple truths: "I am perfectly fine." "This will pass." "I have gotten through this before." You don't have to believe it fully at first. Just keep saying it until it starts to soften the panic.

4. Shrink the moment.
Don't try to solve your whole life at 3 a.m. Just focus on the next five minutes. Breathe. Take a walk. Wash your face. Light a candle. Bring yourself back to the moment you're in.

5. Ask for help.
Whether it's a friend, a therapist, a coach, or a loved one—talking to someone breaks the isolation. You don't have to carry it all in silence.

These aren't magic fixes. But they're places to begin. And sometimes, beginning is everything.

Power to Direct Your Mind

Strength is not never falling apart. It's learning how to gather yourself again with compassion. Life is uncertain. That's a given. But if we let our thoughts tumble into catastrophic fantasies, we'll live in fear—and so will our children.

Take action when you can. Let go when you must. Don't let your mind spin in useless loops that drain your energy and joy.

Moms, this isn't just about your peace of mind; it's about the foundation you're building for your children. When you model mental strength, resilience, and faith, you are gifting them a blueprint for a life of inner peace, no matter what storms they face. You have the power to guide your mind—to calm it, to fill it with light, and to model mental strength for your children. Find what works for you. Practice it. Believe in it. And know that the answers you're looking for are not always out there. Sometimes, they're already within you, waiting for you to simply uncover your own truth.

QUESTIONS TO JOURNAL

- When you fear the future, how do you respond? Does uncertainty create anxiety—or opportunity?
- How does your anxiety show up in your parenting? How does it affect your children?

- What spiritual or mental practices help you stay grounded?
- What consistent habits could you adopt to reduce fear and increase peace?
- What would your life look like if you truly believed the best was yet to come?

> *Emancipate yourself from mental slavery. None but our self can free our minds.*
>
> —Bob Marley

CHAPTER 5

Your Journey, Your Way

Don't shrink your dreams to fit someone else's fears

Life used to be comfortable, and I liked it that way. I wasn't searching for growth or spiritual transformation—I just preferred things to be easy. But when the company my husband and I had built began to crumble, everything else started to unravel with it. In that space of uncertainty, something unexpected emerged: a deeper longing I hadn't known was there.

Every night, during my bath, I'd gaze at the sky and pour out my heart to God, praying for an unshakeable connection. I pleaded for Him to direct my path, to keep me strong, and to guide me to lead the life I was truly meant to lead, untethered from anyone else's expectations.[9]

---

[9] For me this was with my Christian God. For you that might be another tradition or faith. You may even identify more with source or Mother Nature, for example.

Strengthening my spiritual connection helped me get through the season that our preacher always said would happen. He said if we haven't yet gone through a season of suffering, we haven't lived long enough. Well, it took me forty-plus years, and although difficult at the time, the suffering I endured—loss of income, stress over what to do with the company, and marriage-threatening arguments with my husband—was eventually overcome. And like they said would happen, I grew stronger and became a better person. I was also ready to follow God wherever He may lead. I opened my mind and heart so that I could hear what He had to say. Jesus said, "Ask, and you shall receive." So this is what I did—asked God for a closer connection to Him.

I had always assumed that true spiritual connection came through steady devotion—a kind of faithful persistence that would lead to peace and clarity. Then I read something on Yahoo News that shattered that illusion, forcing me to question everything I thought I knew about faith, hope, and even my own journey.

I read this article:

> Mother Teresa: A saint despite spiritual "darkness." When Pope Francis canonizes Mother Teresa on Sunday, he'll be honoring a nun who won admirers around the world and a Nobel Peace Prize for her joy-filled dedication to the "poorest of the poor." He'll also be recognizing holiness in a woman who felt so abandoned by God that she was unable to pray and

was convinced, despite her ever-present smile, that she was experiencing the "tortures of hell."[10]

This revelation didn't just shock me; it profoundly unsettled me. Here was Mother Teresa, the epitome of modern Christian devotion, suffering what she described as the 'tortures of hell' and feeling abandoned by God. If *she*, of all people, couldn't find connection, what hope was there for me, a woman just beginning to seek this elusive bond. The world saw her as a saint, yet her own hidden torments—and the varied perspectives on her work—revealed a stark truth: even the most revered paths are complex, uniquely traveled, and often subject to different interpretations. This forced me to consider how easily we can let another's story, even a saint's, become a perceived barrier to our own.

Just after reading this, my son came into my home office, asking to borrow my car keys. I told him how I had just read this discouraging news about Mother Teresa. He said, "But Mom, everyone is different. You can't assume what she experienced is what you will experience too."

I hadn't thought of it that way. But my son's words offered a profound insight: **we shouldn't let another person's experience dictate our own.** My relationship with God isn't bound by any tradition or expectation. My experience of God is uniquely my own, and I should be free to experience the love and connection that my soul seeks.

---

10 "Mother Teresa: A saint despite spiritual 'darkness'" by Nicole Winfield August 31, 2016; https://www.apnews.com/eb58c9fae2ae441abc040d-6f205b3197

Look at how many people stop going to church because they feel let down by the hypocrisy of regular churchgoers or even the preachers who are supposed to lead the way. But ask yourself, why let other people's behavior interfere with your own or stand in the way of your own path to God or spiritual connection? As Basho said: "Do not seek to follow in the footsteps of the wise. Seek what they sought."

This is true not just for religion, but for anything else you do with your life. Do you not think that too many of us live by the standards that others have set for us—and so limit the available possibilities because we fail to continue to dream? So many times, we fall short of our aspirations because we decide not to pursue our ambitions. We are afraid to expose ourselves to the same difficulties and challenges that we've seen others experience when walking that path. If the statistics are against us or we don't think we have what it takes, then we psych ourselves out. **And more often than not, we give up before we even begin.**

Even when God says, "You can do this! I got your back," we still have our doubts. Like Moses, who taught us *The Ten Commandments*,[11] we let our perceived weaknesses take over and dictate our future, rather than opening our eyes to our potential or playing up our strengths. Moses told God that he has always been "slow of speech and tongue" and didn't have the eloquence required to do His bidding. Even when God reminded him that He was the one who created all men's mouths and could teach him what to say, Moses pleaded with God to send someone else.[12]

---

11 Exodus 20 (KJV)
12 Exodus 4:10 (KJV)

My son, on the other hand, has a different approach. Although he studies the greats, he doesn't let anyone else's experience or what people say get in the way of his dreams. It's tough for my husband and me to let go of our doubts when he doesn't act in a way that we expect or believe is the path to achieving his goals. We open as many doors as we can, but he refuses to go through, as he is focused on a door that only he can see. And when we try to challenge him on his unusual approach and recommend that he spend more time learning from the experience of others, we get nowhere as his response is always the same. He doesn't quote the mythologist Joseph Campbell directly, but it seems to reflect his philosophy of life: "**Follow your bliss and the universe will open doors where there were only walls.**"[13]

My son said, "Mom, what you are criticized for today, you will be praised for tomorrow." He gave me the example of Bill Russell, the Hall of Fame basketball player, who was noted for his unusual style of defensive play. He would jump and block shots but was corrected by his coaches to stay flat-footed at all times so he could react quickly. Now, the number of block-shot defensive moves is an officially tracked statistic in the NBA. Bill Russell did something different, even though it was looked down upon by all the experts, and changed how the game is played.

I don't know yet where my son's thought process will take him. All I can do is hope and pray that his future will be as bright as these famous men, who, despite the odds, worked at what they wanted and continued to believe.

---

13 The Power of Myth by Joseph Campbell (Bantam Doubleday Dell Publishing Group; Reissue Edition, 1989)

- **Jim Carrey**, a high school dropout and janitor who wanted to be a comedian but got booed off the stage during his first stand-up act.
- **Thomas Edison**, labeled by teachers as "too stupid to learn anything," who famously failed 10,000 times to create a light bulb that was economical enough for people to use.
- **Walt Disney**, who dreamed of becoming a good animator but was fired and told he "lacked imagination and had no good ideas."
- **Michael Jordan**, who, after being cut from his high school varsity team, went home, locked himself in his room, and cried.

In 2019's ESPYs award ceremony, a high school football coach named Rob Mendez received the Jimmy V Award for Perseverance. What was remarkable about his achievement was that he led his team through a winning season, only narrowly losing the championship game, despite never having held a football in his hands nor running the length of a football field. He is a successful and inspiring football coach born without any arms or legs. He overcame what for anyone else might have been an insurmountable hurdle, silenced the overwhelming voices of naysayers, and left us with a powerful message on shattering limitations and going after what you believe. In the words of Rob Mendez, he shows us that:

> When you dedicate yourself to something and open your mind to different possibilities and focus on what you can

do instead of what you can't do, you really can go places in this world.[14]

Power to Walk Your Own Path

Most people live by the standards and expectations created by others—parents, peers, teachers, even society at large. Over time, we internalize these limitations and stop questioning whether they still serve us. But the truth is, we don't have to live an ordinary or unfulfilled life just because someone else did.

Moms, we are allowed to dream differently. We're allowed to want more—not just for our kids, but for ourselves. We can pursue meaning, spark creativity, and follow the whispers of our own spiritual path, even if no one else understands it. When you embrace your own distinct path—whether spiritual, creative, or professional—you not only reclaim your joy, but you also show your children, in the most profound way, what it truly means to live a life unconstrained by external fears and expectations. You teach them that their own whispers of purpose are worth listening to.

It takes courage to follow a voice no one else can hear. But that's what transformation requires. It begins when you trust what's inside you more than what surrounds you. And when you give yourself that freedom, you model it for your children too.

---

14 https://www.today.com/news/rob-mendez-football-coach-no-arms-or-legs-delivers-speech-t158158

QUESTIONS TO JOURNAL

- Have you ever held yourself back because of someone else's story? Do you want your child to behave in the same way?
- How can you clarify what you want, not what others expect of you?
- Are you unknowingly passing on limiting beliefs to your children?
- What could be possible if your child followed their dream—no matter how unconventional?

> Whether you think you can or think you can't, either way you're right.
>
> —Henry Ford

CHAPTER 6

Leading From Within

Inner Power Is Stronger Than Willpower

At a women's power retreat that my company sponsored, I volunteered for a hypnosis session. I'd never tried it before. As it turned out, my mind was too alert, too resistant—I couldn't be fully hypnotized. But what stayed with me wasn't the hypnosis itself; it was what the hypnotist said as she began the induction.

"You are not your thoughts," she whispered gently. "Thoughts will drift through your mind. Let them come. Let them go. Don't grab hold. *They are not you.*"

That single sentence reshaped something fundamental in me. Until then, I'd assumed every thought—even the dark, intrusive ones—had something to say about me. But this idea, that I could observe my thoughts without being defined by them, was revolutionary. It gave me language for something I had long sensed but never articulated: **there is a deeper me beneath the noise, a truer self, untouched by the fleeting currents of my mind.**

You Are Not Your Thoughts

There are certain times when negative thoughts seem to gain more power—moments when our emotional defenses are lower and our minds feel more vulnerable. As women, our moods can be influenced by a complex interplay of hormones, stress, and the weight of responsibilities. During these moments, I sometimes feel an overwhelming sense of doom, irritability, or quickness to anger. But thankfully, I'd already begun to understand that these thoughts weren't me—they were merely visitors.

How many of our children—especially teenagers—understand this? How many of them are tormented by their thoughts, mistaking them for truth? I wish someone had told me sooner: intrusive thoughts are not character flaws. They're just noise. And as long as we don't act on them, we are not defined by them. **We are not the voice of our minds—we are just the listener.**

There's a quiet force within each of us—a sacred inner awareness that watches without judgment, calmly witnessing the storm of our thoughts. This deeper self is where our true strength resides. When we nourish this awareness and allow it to lead, our beliefs begin to reflect its clarity and peace. And from those beliefs, our thoughts follow. As Gandhi said, "Your beliefs become your thoughts, your thoughts become your words, your words become your actions." When we feed the spirit, we don't just change our minds—we transform our lives.

I've experienced firsthand the immense power of this inner awareness. It has shifted the way I see myself and how I move through the world. It hasn't made me perfect, but it has helped me step away from the version of myself I no longer wanted to be—and closer to the person I was always meant to become.

A Mother's Rage

For many years, I was angry. The kind of anger that didn't live in me all the time, but surged in those pressured, overloaded moments—when the demands of work, parenting, and life collided, and I felt like I was stretched beyond my limits. When my kids resisted my instructions, stalled on homework, or refused dinner, I snapped. I yelled. I lost control. Once, in frustration, I even tried to force food into my daughter's mouth. Another time, I screamed at my son for turning a simple homework assignment into a two-hour ordeal. And when I'd finally fall into bed, hoping for peace, I'd hear a little voice calling, "Moaam!"—never "Dad"—and I'd break. "WHAT DO YOU WANT?!" I would shout, utterly drained, running on empty, with nothing left to give.

Looking back, I ask myself: where did all that fury come from?

I had a loving childhood. I grew up in a warm Caribbean home with no major trauma, no missing pieces. We had helpers who cooked, cleaned, did laundry, and tended the garden. I never had to take on responsibilities beyond school, piano, swimming, tennis lessons, and the occasional chore. Perhaps that was part of the problem. My life had been so easy, so insulated from responsibility, that the weight of motherhood hit like a tidal wave. And maybe, too, it came from being painfully shy. For so many years, I wanted to chat freely and socialize like a regular kid, but I was too afraid to open my mouth. I didn't trust that I could speak in coherent sentences unless I rehearsed what I would say in advance. I kept so much bottled up. Maybe my adult rage was simply the dam breaking.

I thought this explained my anger until I came across a passage from the book *Little Fires Everywhere* by Celeste Ng: *"Though she would never quite articulate it this way, resentment began to sheathe concern.* ANGER IS FEAR'S BODYGUARD," a poster in the hospital had read.[15]

I was afraid for my kids—afraid of what might become of them if they didn't succeed in school, in sports, or in life. I feared for myself, too—that I was being asked to give more than I had, that I would fail them and myself. Anger had risen up inside me as a shield, masking the fear that I didn't want to feel.

Most of the time, I'm cool and collected. But with my kids, I would lose control. Until my younger son was diagnosed, I had no idea that ADHD could present as inattentiveness without hyperactivity. My sons didn't run around wildly or bounce off walls. They could sit still—but their minds would wander, especially during homework. When I tried to help, they laughed at the wrong moments, which felt deeply disrespectful in my already frayed state.

To make it worse, they often did the opposite of what I asked. I'd explain something clearly—like aligning equal signs when solving math problems to make the steps easier to follow—and they would intentionally misalign them. Even when they saw

---

15 *Little Fires Everywhere* by Celeste Ng (Little, Brown, 2017)

my frustration bubbling over, they kept pushing. I now believe some of it was intentional resistance, but some was also their own way of coping with the pressure to focus—and with me.

With my daughter, it was different. She grasped things quickly but refused to follow my agenda. She wanted control over her timing, her decisions. This defiance triggered escalating power struggles until I finally learned to let go and allow her to experience the consequences of her choices.

Their behavior—rebellious, defiant, and at times, dismissive—made me feel like a victim. And in that victimhood, I gave myself permission to retaliate with rage, shouting until my voice was hoarse, my words sharp as knives tearing down their confidence and my own. But no matter what challenges our children present, we never have the right to take our emotions out on them. I knew that then, and I know it even more clearly now.

Taking Control

I realized that I needed to get control of myself. I would watch *Supernanny*, talk shows, or read parenting books, including one titled *ScreamFree Parenting* by Hal Edward Runkel. They all made sense but didn't seem to address my problem, which was that as soon as the spark was lit, the fire would burn until there was a massive explosion. I would regret getting angry as soon as it was over, but I didn't know how to stop the immediate reaction. Someone could tell me how bad an effect it was having on my kids until I was blue in the face, but it wouldn't have made a difference. My understanding that it was wrong was not enough to stop it from happening again. I knew I needed a circuit breaker, but where was it? What could stop this from happening again and again?

I had no idea, but I knew this behavior wasn't me. This wasn't who I was or wanted to be. Something else was taking over my body and causing it to behave in ways that were shocking and outrageous to me. I had had enough. The real "me" was at a loss for correcting this problem and was crying out for help. I didn't know what else to do. The only thing left was to turn to God, and so I started to pray. This wasn't a quiet, composed prayer. It was guttural, pleading, unfiltered. I cried out with every fiber of my being, begging for help. And for the first time in my life, I came to truly understand and experience the power of prayer. It was the only thing that could transform me. And it did.

In the heat of the next confrontation, I noticed a new sensation—a flicker of awareness, like someone watching from the inside. That presence, quiet and steady, gave me just enough space to pause. And in that moment, I found a way to pull myself back from the edge. Over time, the gap widened. The anger didn't vanish, but it lost its grip. My wiser self—the woman I was trying to become—began to step forward.

Prayer opened the door. But awareness is what helped me walk through it.

I'm not saying I no longer get angry. I still do. But now I have more control. That flash of awareness—the observer—shows up sooner. Within a second or two, I can reset, breathe, and choose not to go off track. I'm no longer at the mercy of the outer, reactive self. I've learned to let my inner woman lead.

Once I adopted a calmer, more rational parenting approach—the one I describe in Chapter 2—I stopped setting myself up for explosive moments. I wasn't forcing everything to go my way. I allowed room for flexibility, for grace. And that made it sustainable. It's what carried me through the hardest seasons of parenting.

Three Life-Changing Habits

Through this journey, I discovered three profound truths—three sources of power—that reshaped my life and helped me become not just a better mother, but a more grounded, spiritually aware woman.

1. The Power of Prayer

The first is really incredible: to know that prayer works! Prayer is not just asking for something—it's surrendering to something greater than yourself. It's not about resisting *what is* but embracing it so deeply that you allow your soul to speak its truest longing. When you pray from that place, something begins to move—within you and around you.

This made me think of a recent conversation I had with a friend about baptism by water. I always thought of the water being used primarily as a symbol to cleanse people of their sins to be born anew. I believe St. Paul also referred to the act of being submerged in water as like going down into the grave and then coming out as if resurrected. My friend, who is not a Christian, believes you get to know God only through your own experience. He explained that when you are underwater, you cannot breathe, there is no other thought in your head, no suffering, no challenges, no problems—only one thing matters: to rise to the surface and fill your lungs with air. So, it is with that singular focus that you can experience God—when nothing else matters but Him.

That's how I think of prayer. When you don't just knock, but you bang on the door—**because your soul knows there is no other way out—that's when the door will be opened for you.**

As the wise king in *The Alchemist* said, **"When you want something, all the universe conspires in helping you to achieve it."**[16] I believe that's true—but only when what you want aligns with your truest, deepest self.

2. The Power of the Observer

The second power I discovered is the witness within—an awareness, a presence, a calm consciousness that watches without judgment. It's always been there, but I hadn't truly noticed it until one morning when I was driving to work along the San Mateo Bridge.

I didn't want to go to work. My baby son was with my aunt, and what I longed for was a quiet day at home to spend with him. Driving across the bridge, I spotted a rainbow—something about it felt like a sign. I kept staring at it, distracted, until I looked down and saw nothing but red break lights on the cars in front. It was too late. *I was going to crash.*

---

16 *The Alchemist* by Paulo Coelho (HarperTorch; International ed. Edition, 2006)

Instinctively, I swerved right. Miraculously, the lane was empty—unusual for a weekday morning. But now I was headed straight into the guardrail. I swerved again, this time to the left, but there was nothing more I could do. The barrier was coming fast—and I was going to hit it.

And then time slowed.

In those split seconds, something shifted. I became the observer—calm, detached, watching myself brace for impact. I noticed the type of barrier, calculated the odds of surviving the crash, and waited. My car bounced off a rubber edge and spun around to face oncoming traffic. The accident made the Bay Area news. I walked away unscathed—but inside, something had awakened.

Time had stretched, as if the universe gave me space to see everything more clearly. I've since learned that many people describe this same sensation just before a crash—the slowing down, the hyper-awareness, the sense that something else takes over. In that stillness, a voice emerged—not panicked or urgent, but steady and clear.

In that moment, I discovered the observer—the unwavering voice that can rise above fear. Since then, I've tried to access her in everyday life. She's not dramatic or loud. She's quiet, guiding me back to calm when things fall apart. She reminds me that I don't have to react—I can respond. I don't have to be afraid—I can choose peace.

I sometimes imagine the observer as my better self—one who sees everything clearly and moves through life without fear. That's the version of me I strive to live as: the one who waits before yelling, breathes before blaming, listens before leaping. That voice helps me stay rooted in truth and guided by spirit.

I believe this is what Jesus meant when he said, *"The kingdom of God is within you."* That still, sacred place inside—free from anger, ego, or fear—is where divine presence lives.

In Oprah Winfrey's book, *The Path Made Clear*, Gary Zukav describes how to pause and go inside to find your "authentic power" rather than just react when you're feeling frustrated, overwhelmed, or angry with your kids. He says:

> Because just by turning inward instead of acting in the moment you have created a little gap between the impulse and the action. And into that space, you can inject consciousness. [...] you can do something you couldn't have done before.[17]

3. *The Power of Self-awareness*

Without self-awareness, we live on autopilot—reacting instead of responding, cycling through the same emotional loops without understanding why. Every minor inconvenience feels like a crisis. People who don't act the way we expect begin to irritate us. We feel overwhelmed, frustrated, and stuck.

It's like being a hamster on a wheel—running endlessly, trapped in patterns we can't break. The same arguments, the same stress, the same emotional explosions repeat again and again.

---

17 *The Path Made Clear* by Oprah Winfrey (Bluebird, 2019)

But when we tap into self-awareness, something shifts. We start to *see* ourselves. We begin to observe our thoughts instead of becoming them. We notice our triggers, our habits, our emotional undercurrents—and in that noticing, we reclaim our power.

With this awareness, we can take a step back. We can make a different choice. We can speak calmly instead of yelling, reflect instead of lashing out, release instead of controlling.

Self-awareness doesn't mean you'll never get upset again. It means you won't stay lost in it. You'll know how to find your way back.

It is the key to both personal and spiritual growth. When we live with conscious awareness, we aren't dragged down by every irritation. We become more spacious, more forgiving, more able to evolve into the best version of ourselves.

Bringing About Personal Change

I'm not a spiritual teacher or a guru. I'm just a mother who was desperate enough to ask for help—and willing enough to listen when an answer came. I still have to work at it *every single day*. What worked for me may not work for you. For me, it was prayer. For others, it may be meditation, yoga, therapy, mindfulness, or a different spiritual practice. There is no single path—only the one that helps you find your way back to yourself.

Here are a few steps in the process that can help bring about change and enable you to find your own power:

You are not your thoughts. Don't confuse a dark thought with a dark heart. You are not your mistakes, your impulses, or the worst thing you've ever thought or done in frustration. Realize that there is a "true you" that is separate and distinct from the outer person or the ego that has been masquerading as you and leading you down the wrong path. There is a deeper you—stronger, wiser, and untouched by all of it. Get to know her.

Don't identify with your pain. There are parts of you that were shaped by hard experiences, by trauma, by upbringing. See them for what they are—parts of your ego and your human state. Think of these as chapters in your story, not the book of who you truly are, nor part of your core identity. Your ego might act out, because of what has built up over time, but that's not your essence. You are not broken. You are becoming.

Listen for the observer. You've likely heard her already. She's that still voice who notices you losing control—without judgment. She might show up in a quiet moment, when your anger has reached a boiling point or when you are too exhausted to think. Pause. Invite her in. Give her the mic. Let her lead.

Believe in the power within. This shift isn't just possible—it's already beginning. If you give it a chance, you'll discover that the power inside you is stronger than your thoughts, stronger than your fear, stronger even than your will. Miraculous change begins the moment you trust it.

Keep your spirit in charge. Even after awakening, the ego doesn't retire quietly. It will try to reclaim its throne with old habits and self-doubt. But when you remember your values, your vision, and the woman you are becoming, you reclaim control. Do not give in to a lesser version of yourself. Instead, allow the observer, your higher consciousness, to be the force that propels you forward to the life you are meant to lead.

When you let your ego lead, life feels heavy and full of struggle. But **when you let your spirit guide you, something shifts—life starts to feel aligned, peaceful, and purposeful.**

Power to Change

Most people are only motivated to change when they hit rock bottom. Even though you may not have reached that point, you know when you should take the opportunity to choose a different, far better road.

You don't have to wait until everything breaks down to rise up. The doorway to change is always open. Sometimes it just takes exhaustion, or exasperation, or one final straw to make you walk through it.

When you feel like you've tried everything—books, advice, effort—and still nothing works, don't give up. Reach inward. Reach higher. Speak to God. Call on the universe. Ask boldly, honestly, vulnerably. That cry is not weakness—it's power. And it can summon the strength already inside you.

Moms, if your outer self is creating chaos within yours and your children's lives, let your inner self take the lead. That quiet, steady voice knows the way. Listen for it. Trust it. Follow it. Because **you are not your thoughts. You are the power behind them.**

QUESTIONS TO JOURNAL

- The next time you get angry or lose control, imagine it's being recorded. Play it back in your mind—watch your tone, your body language, your energy. Is this who you want to be? Is this the example you want to set?

- When you pause and view yourself from the outside—as the observer—what do you see? In those moments of rising tension, what small shift could help you regain control? (Deep breaths, stepping away, counting to ten, repeating a mantra?)

- Is your intention clear, honest, and grounded in love? If so, try one more thing: call on a higher power, however you define it. Ask sincerely, from your heart. Then listen.

- Think back to a moment when your fear or anger softened because you connected to your higher self. What changed in you? Did peace enter the moment? Did things begin to flow more easily?

Sometimes you don't realize your own strength until you come face to face with your greatest weakness.

—Susan Gale

CHAPTER 7

Expanding Perspective

*When you let go of being right,
you begin to see more clearly*

The parable of the Blind Men and the Elephant tells of six blind men encountering an elephant for the first time. Each touches a different part—its side, trunk, tusk, leg, ear, and tail—and draws a wildly different conclusion. To one, the elephant is like a wall; to another, a snake, a spear, a tree, a fan, or a rope. The parable concludes: "Each in his own opinion, exceeding stiff and strong, though each was partly in the right, and all were in the wrong."[18]

Traditionally, this parable serves as a caution against religious absolutism—a reminder that no single person can grasp the full truth. But to me, its message is even broader. It's a call to humility. A reminder that our perspectives are always limited by our experiences, and that truth in this world is rarely singular, often a composite of many viewpoints. We each see a sliver of the picture. We must speak our truth, yes—but not impose it. We must

---

18 https://en.wikisource.org/wiki/The_poems_of_John_Godfrey_Saxe/The_Blind_Men_and_the_Elephant

be open to what others see, even when it's different from our own.

Differing Views

My husband and I grew up worlds apart. He was raised in London, the son of a bus driver and a nurse. He tells stories of being the only child on the block without a bicycle, of standing at windows watching other children eat dinner while waiting outside with his soccer ball for them to come out and play.

I, on the other hand, grew up in Jamaica, the daughter of two doctors. We lived in a beautiful neighborhood in Kingston with mango trees, a tennis court, a cricket pitch, and a gully with a river running through the back. I have memories of surprise trips to Disney World, being picked up from school mid-day by my dad with warm beef patties in hand. My siblings and I are still incredibly close, something I credit to my selfless, loving mother and the family-centered life our parents created.

Inevitably, our differing worlds meant we would clash on how to raise our own children. Take vacations, for example. For me, they're sacred—one of the few times we can break out of routine and reconnect as a family. But my husband sees them as a luxury that the kids haven't earned. He runs kids' sports camps, so school holidays are his busiest time. Getting him to take a vacation with the family is next to impossible. As a result, the kids and I often travel without him—and that's where tension begins.

The central battleground? Whether our adult son, who wasn't in school or working, should be included. Was I spoiling him, or as my husband says, "rewarding him," for something he doesn't deserve? That is one way of looking at it. I've continued to take him on some trips, not as a reward, but because I believe in the power of shared experience. Vacations create moments—hanging out at the beach, going on rides, sightseeing—that simply don't happen in the grind of daily life. They allow siblings to bond, create lifelong memories, and experience something larger than themselves.

I understand my husband's concern. I've adjusted. I no longer take our son on every trip. But when it's a once-in-a-lifetime opportunity—like our recent European adventure—or a gathering with extended family, I do. And I've seen the positive effects. After Europe, my son told me the trip "opened his eyes." It boosted his confidence and showed him a world beyond what he knew.

For other, more routine trips, I ask him to sit them out or pay his own way. It's a compromise I can live with. He gets the message but still benefits from meaningful experiences. My husband disagrees. To him, it's simple: no job, no reward. I get that. But I believe we can send the message in ways that don't involve sacrificing precious family moments.

But it wasn't easy to come up with a resolution that worked for both of us. I wrestled with the guilt, the judgment, and the fear that I was failing in my role. I often felt like I was standing alone—trying to hold on to a value I cherished, while being told it was wrong. It wasn't just a disagreement; it felt personal. Deep.

Wins and Losses

'Agree to disagree' works in theory, but in a marriage—especially when it comes to raising children—it's a temporary truce. Eventually, a real decision needs to be made. Then someone has to yield—or push forward. And that can be hard.

Most parents have deeply held views about what's best for their kids. So what happens when those views conflict? Who leads? Who follows? Who decides?

Some turn to scripture, where passages describe the man as the head of the household. I'm not that kind of Christian. I embrace the teachings of Christ, but I don't take everything literally.

And truthfully, it's exhausting—this back and forth. The tug-of-war between what I feel is right and what he insists is best. Sometimes I wonder if we'll ever fully understand each other when it comes to parenting—or if we'll always feel like we're fighting for something no one else sees.

Parenting Approaches

Early on, parenting differences may not seem like a big deal. One parent takes the lead on daily decisions. But as children grow and challenges arise, so do the stakes. That's when the tension begins to build.

In many households, parenting roles tend to fall into patterns—but those patterns vary widely. In some families, the father may lean more toward enforcing rules, while the mother focuses on nurturing. In others, the roles are reversed—or shared. What's important isn't the pattern itself, but how the differences are acknowledged and respected.

A small moment can reveal a big difference in parenting styles. One morning after Valentine's Day, I was enjoying a rare slow start when my husband jolted awake. It was 8:30 a.m. Our younger son had school. My husband swore under his breath and rushed to get ready.

He and our son had a routine. Tired of nagging the kids to get ready, he told them: call me only when you're fully ready to leave. And if they weren't ready on time and would be late for school, he'd drop them off at the bottom of the hill outside the school grounds—and they'd have to walk the rest of the way.

That morning, I heard him shout downstairs, "You know what this means, right? You're walking up the hill."

Our son sighed, "Yeah, I know. I thought Mom would be up. She usually is."

On hearing this conversation, I immediately looked out the window to see if it was raining. There'd been a storm for the past three days, and it rained all night, so I was concerned my son would get soaked walking up the hill. I didn't want him to get sick because we were flying to Portland that night for a major basketball tournament. But I let it go. Because I knew: the consequence had to stick. Rules mean little if we don't follow through. So even if it was raining outside, my son had to grab a jacket and walk up the hill.

Acknowledging Differences

If mom and dad can recognize and acknowledge their differences yet see the value in both styles of parenting, then their children will end up receiving the best of both worlds. Parents that respect each other can discuss and agree upon a decision that they are both comfortable with and can consistently follow an approach.

On the other hand, disrespecting the other parent's view can have negative consequences. Just because your co-parent has different opinions doesn't mean they are wrong. So provided your partner has the child's best interest at heart and is not pushing their own agenda out of selfishness or malice, stop and listen—and encourage them to do the same. Each person should recognize their limitations, understand one person is not always right, and let the other person's perspective enlarge their own.

Since I've spent so many years in the corporate world, I can't help but see parallels between team decision-making and parenting decisions. In software, when you're deciding on the next big release, there is often disagreement on which features should be prioritized. As a product director, your job is to guide the team through a structured process to make the best call with the information you have. Then you execute, observe, and adjust.

In parenting, we can take a similar approach, as outlined in the following table:

	PRODUCTS	CHILDREN
The core question	Which features to release first for the most significant impact on the market?	Which parenting action will deliver the best outcome for the child?
Know your customer/ child	What drives them, who influences them, their preferences and habits, their buying behavior, etc.	What drives them, who influences them, their strengths and weaknesses, preferences and habits, past behavior, etc.
Evaluate opinions/ discuss options	Consider market trends, customer input, competitors, company strategy, sales potential, and cost.	Each parent explains their perspective, while the other parent listens with empathy—and without judgment. Parents should recognize they share the same goal and take care to acknowledge the values that matter most to each other. Expert advice may be considered, although one parent may trust experts more than the other.
Make a decision	Typically, the product leader decides with executive approval.	Ideally, both parents agree. If not, the parent who feels more strongly may lead. The other may acquiesce—this time.

EXPANDING PERSPECTIVE

Execute on the decision	Deliver the chosen features to the market with confidence.	Stick with the decision. Mixed messages create loopholes kids will exploit.
Evaluate the outcome	How many new users or customers? What's the return on investment?	Observe your child's behavior and well-being. If no positive change occurs, reassess.
Iterate as needed	Faster cycles, leads to quicker feedback and better products.	Don't cling to what doesn't work. Be willing to adapt, learn, and try a new approach.

There is power in merging thoughts and ideas and bringing together the best of multiple perspectives, rather than fighting each other to determine who is right. If the six blind men were open to and listened to each other's perspective, they would finally realize the complete picture of the elephant.

Inner Compass

The truth is, nothing in life is "cookie-cutter." It's been a massive challenge for us to agree on a parenting approach. I can't control my husband, but I'm learning to control myself. Still, it hasn't been easy. One of the hardest parts was confronting my own defensiveness. If I was doing what felt deeply, intuitively right—how could it be wrong?

That question haunted me. My parenting choices weren't careless; they were deliberate, rooted in love and what I believed was right. So when those choices were criticized—by my husband, by my children—I felt gutted. It didn't just sting; it felt like a betrayal of my core self to even consider doing things differently. Was I supposed to ignore my instincts? Abandon what had always guided me?

Parenting shook me to the core. Although I've always been shy, I've also always been clear about who I am and what I want. I've pursued big goals and often succeeded. But in parenting, that clarity vanished. I felt like I was walking on shifting ground, no longer sure of what was right or wrong. My gut, which had once been my compass, now led me in circles.

But being wrong about something that feels instinctively right doesn't mean you've lost your way—it means you're being invited to grow. I've realized that not everything that feels natural is aligned with truth. Much of what we call "instinct" is actually shaped by past experience and unconscious patterns. My gut said to give, to rescue, to soften every hard edge. That wasn't wisdom. That was programming.

I used to equate my parenting style with who I am—as if changing my approach meant abandoning myself. But it didn't. Letting go of what wasn't working wasn't a betrayal of who I am. It meant letting go of a method that wasn't working, so I could become the mother they actually needed.

I was raised by loving parents who gave me everything, and still, I had ambition. I knew I had to leave Jamaica, move to the U.S., and build a life on my own. So I assumed my kids would eventually crave that same independence. But they are not me. Their timelines and truths are their own.

There's a difference between instinct and inner wisdom. Instinct is loud and urgent. Wisdom is still and steady. Letting go of assumptions opens space for clarity—and often, unexpected grace. **Sometimes, the ground has to fall away before you realize there's a deeper foundation waiting beneath your feet.** The answer doesn't lie only in your own viewpoint—but also in the perspectives of those you love.

Power to See

The year 2020 was like no other. It caused us to upend our comfortable lives, alter our routines, and forced us to stretch ourselves in ways that we would never have imagined. It also presented an unprecedented opportunity to expand our perspective and to grow. Social injustice and inequities were impossible to ignore, driving people of all races and walks of life to acknowledge and appreciate the experiences of those less privileged, less fortunate, or different. On the other hand, politics, especially in the US, polarized and divided us, making it difficult to comprehend the mindsets of those on the other side. If we can learn to treat others with empathy, compassion, and understanding in the worst of times, we will practice it in the best of times, and do our part to unite our families, our communities, and the world.

This is where your unique power as a mother comes in. Moms, you have the power to do something that many others may not. You can show by example, how to quiet your voice and mind when the other person is speaking and listen without judgment. By focusing your full attention on your partner or child, you will open yourself to truly hearing what they have to say and may begin to see things in a new light. When you connect with someone in this manner, not only will you gain perspective, but they will sense the power of your presence, and your words will have a greater impact when it is your turn to speak.

QUESTIONS TO JOURNAL

- When your spouse, co-parent, or teenager has a strong opinion that's different from yours, do you judge them for it? Do you think something is wrong with them and wish they would change?
- Do you hold on tightly to your perspective because you believe it defines who you are?
- The next time you get into a heated argument, pause and put yourself in the other person's shoes—even if they never do that for you. Are you surprised by what you discover?
- When you show that you understand where someone is coming from, even if you disagree, how does it change the conversation?

> **When you change the way you look at things, the things you look at change.**
>
> —Wayne Dyer

CHAPTER 8

Defusing Conflict

*If You're Strong on the Inside,
There's No Need to Fight*

A few years ago, during a job interview, I was asked a question intended to gauge culture fit with the company : "Name a character in a book, tv show or movie—real or fictional—you most admire. What is it about them that inspires you?"

Without much time to think, I answered instinctively: "Chief Inspector Armand Gamache of the Sûreté du Québec" from Louise Penny's mystery novels.

Gamache isn't like the other detectives in his squad. While his team often dives headfirst into facts and timelines, he often steps away—to walk in the woods, to reflect in silence. It's in those quiet moments that his real insight emerges. I admire that deeply. As someone who also finds creating space allows new ideas to rise, I recognize the power in this process. But what truly inspires me about Gamache is not just his intellect, but his emotional wisdom.

He leads with calm, with empathy, and with four simple phrases that he teaches to every new recruit:

> I was wrong.
>
> I'm sorry.
>
> I don't know.
>
> I need help.[19]

Imagine if more people lived by that code. How many arguments could be avoided, how many relationships healed, if we all had the humility and inner strength to say those words?

Why it's So Hard to Say the Simple Things

Those four phrases sound so simple. But in real life—especially in marriage—they can feel nearly impossible to say.

Not because we don't mean them, but because our egos get in the way. When we're caught in conflict, it's easy to believe we're arguing about the situation itself—who did what, or who's being unreasonable. But underneath, we're often fighting to feel seen, respected, or understood.

This was certainly true in my own marriage. A simple request—like asking me to stop by the store—could turn tense in seconds

---

19 https://www.louisepenny.com/

when I was already overwhelmed from juggling work, kids, and the mental load of running a household. Many nights, I'd get messages like this on my drive home:

> **Husband:** Can you stop by the store to pick up a bottle of wine?
>
> **Me:** Sorry, I don't have time. Kids are in the car. I have to get home to do laundry and work on my presentation for Monday. Can you please get it yourself?
>
> **Husband:** I understand. I thought I was asking for something simple, but apparently not.
>
> **Me:** You are something else. A little understanding and consideration would be nice. If it's that simple, why can't you get it?
>
> **Husband:** Just forget it. Sorry, I asked.

Neither of us was trying to start a fight. But we were both reacting from emotion and unspoken expectations. I felt maxed out, unacknowledged for everything I was already handling. He felt dismissed and frustrated. And just like that, we were in a standoff over something that wasn't even about wine.

We were each defending our own sense of fairness and emotional truth—both of us trying to protect ourselves, not realizing or caring that we were hurting each other in the process.

Over time, these small breakdowns created emotional distance. I'd often revisit the disagreement the next day, hoping to explain where I was coming from or clear the air. But my husband would say he had already moved on. He didn't want to relive the moment. I didn't want to leave it unresolved. We were stuck in a painful loop—me reaching for repair, him pulling away to protect peace.

Our marriage was strong in many ways. We loved each other, laughed together, and showed up for our family. But when conflict entered the room, it could cloud everything good. We always found our way back, but I longed for more—not just a return to normal, but a deeper sense of being understood.

Eventually, a much bigger disagreement involving the kids and my husband's business forced us to break the pattern. This time, the impact was too big to sweep aside. I insisted we go to family counseling, and thankfully, we did.

Sitting in a room with a third party gave us something we hadn't been able to find on our own: space to speak honestly, and to truly listen. It wasn't about assigning blame or fixing each other. **It was about remembering that we were on the same side.**

The healing didn't begin because everything was solved—it began because we stopped trying to win and started trying to understand.

Teamwork

Even after counseling helped reset our family dynamic, the tension between my husband and me didn't fully go away. He continued to feel unsupported. I continued to feel unfairly criticized—especially when it came to money and parenting decisions. These patterns ran deep, and they rose to the surface right before the holidays.

My extended family was visiting us in California, and I had bought generous Christmas gifts for everyone. I'd also covered much of the cost of the upcoming ski trip in Tahoe for the kids and me. From my perspective, it was a joyful and well-deserved splurge. But for my husband, the contrast between what he saw as "lavish" spending and our pending business start-up costs was just too much. The tipping point came when I asked him to come with me to buy our son's gift—and to pay for it.

To me, it was a straightforward equation. I cover more than half of our household and family expenses. The remaining balance, in my mind, was his responsibility. But no matter how clearly I laid out the numbers, my logic never seemed to land. I'd tally up receipts, explain the percentages, show it all in black and white—but it wasn't a language he wanted to speak.

And that's when I realized: this wasn't about math. It was about meaning. About what money represents. About how we each measure value, fairness, and support.

Around that time, I happened to watch an episode of *Red Table Talk*, where Jada Pinkett Smith interviewed Jay Shetty, a former monk turned motivational speaker.[20] What he said was an eye-opener:

> "If we don't see that we are a team, then we are going to lose every time. Together. 'Cause you winning and me

---

20 https://www.facebook.com/watch/?v=660056184408432

losing is still a loss for us both. Winning together is the priority."

That was exactly what we had been missing. We weren't seeing each other as teammates—we were tallying separate scorecards.

I'd spent years in the corporate world, leading and collaborating across teams. My husband, as the president of his own company, hadn't had the same need to accommodate or adjust to others. He liked to point out that his years playing soccer made him more of a team player than I'd ever be as a tennis player. But as the lead striker and top goal scorer, he was used to being the one everyone else passed the ball to. In our marriage, I had started to feel like the rest of the team—always assisting, never seen as an equal on the field.

Things finally erupted after one last comment he made about gifts, vacations, and spoiling the kids. I'd been holding it all in, trying to make it through the holidays. But in that moment, I couldn't stay silent anymore. I told him—calmly but clearly—that even though I loved him, I couldn't keep living under a cloud of criticism. I needed something to change.

And he listened. This time, he didn't interrupt or argue. He just took it in. And when I finished, he quietly said, "Sometimes you don't realize what you do that contributes to the problem."

He was right. I hadn't been playing as a teammate either. I had been leading with logic instead of compassion—defending my decisions instead of nurturing our relationship. That night, I made a decision. I chose to stop measuring who was right or fair or justified. I chose him. I chose *us*.

My husband is a good, loving man. I feel safe in his arms, grounded in his presence. Even though I knew we'd still disagree sometimes—especially around fairness or money—I realized that being right wasn't worth more than what we had built together.

I can't fully explain what shifted that day, but something real and lasting did. I had been on the edge of giving up. But instead, our marriage changed—radically and for the better. We softened. We listened. We gave each other more grace. The threat of loss had made us remember what we stood to lose—and it gave us the will to protect what mattered most.

Resolving Conflict

Kindness and empathy are what keep a marriage healthy—not just during the good times, but in moments of disagreement. In fact, research has shown that kindness—paired with emotional stability—is the strongest predictor of a lasting, happy partnership.[21] But in day-to-day life, it's not just love that keeps us afloat. It's our ability to manage conflict before it swells and capsizes everything else.

For a long time, I didn't understand how much my own passion for fairness was contributing to the tension in our home. I believed that if something was unjust or irrational, I had to call it out. I couldn't let things go—not until the other person acknowledged I was right. I clung to my arguments like a dog

---

21 https://www.theatlantic.com/health/archive/2014/06/happily-ever-after/372573/

with a bone, desperately hoping that if I explained myself clearly enough, my husband and my kids would eventually agree.

But they never did. Especially not in the heat of the moment.

Eventually, I had to face a hard truth: repeating myself didn't make me more persuasive—it just made me easier to tune out. I was creating more pressure, not resolution. These days, I speak my truth once—clearly and calmly—and then I stop. Ironically, that's a more assertive position because it comes from a place of inner strength, not a desperate need to control. And without all the added friction, tensions don't inflate like a balloon waiting to burst.

I've also learned that I don't have to react to everything. If my husband says something I find unfair or off-base, I don't have to launch into a counterargument. I can pause. Let it slide. Let him have his experience. **I've stopped trying to control the story in his head, because I've grown more confident in my own.**

A big reason I used to engage in conflict was self-protection. Like a porcupine, I'd raise my quills when my ego felt threatened. Especially when it came to parenting. If my husband or kids criticized something I did, I took it personally—as if it meant I wasn't a good mother. And that fear made me defensive. I'd argue not because I was always right, but because I was trying to shield myself from shame.

But over time, I realized that my parenting choices weren't a reflection of my worth—they were a reflection of my experience, my learning, and my humanity. Yes, I've made mistakes. We all do. But I've also acted out of love, and that matters more. Once I accepted that, I didn't need to defend myself anymore. I knew who I was—and I didn't need anyone else to confirm it for me.

And here's the beautiful part: when I stopped reacting with sharp edges, something shifted in those around me. When I didn't raise my quills, they didn't raise theirs either.

It was my daughter who drove that point home. She once quoted Wayne Dyer[22] to me:

"Conflict cannot survive without your participation."

For the most part she tries to live by that principle. When someone lashes out, she gives them space. "People don't mean the hurtful things they say," she told me once. "They're just blowing off steam. If you stay silent, they'll stop and think. And then, they'll usually feel a little stupid."

And you know what? She's right. It works. My mother taught me something similar years earlier—in a more practical way. During an argument between my daughter and me at a Paris café, my mother leaned in and said, "When your children are being disrespectful, stop talking. Let them figure it out." That, too, turned out to be great advice.

Like a cold, behavior is contagious. When one person changes their response, others eventually do too. Our family still has deep conversations and strong disagreements, but they rarely

---

22 https://www.goodreads.com/quotes/76465-conflict-cannot-survive-without-your-participation

turn into emotional battles. We've learned how to let things pass instead of escalate. And the result is a home that feels calmer, lighter, and more peaceful.

Transforming Conflict into Kindness

What surprised me most was how removing just one habit—engaging in unnecessary conflict—completely shifted the dynamic of our marriage. It was like discovering that one ingredient had been overpowering the entire dish. Once it was gone, the whole flavor of our relationship changed. Everything tasted lighter, brighter, more balanced.

I see my husband in a different light—and I know he sees me differently too. We're communicating, relating, and connecting in ways I didn't know were possible. It's a gift I wish I had unwrapped twenty years ago. But perhaps if I had, I wouldn't be writing this book or sharing this hard-earned wisdom with you now.

The truth is, disagreements will always happen. But conflict doesn't have to define your relationship—at least not when it's grounded in mutual love and respect. What matters isn't avoiding conflict altogether but learning how to move through it with maturity and grace.

Here are a few practices that have helped me transform conflict into connection:

1. **Wait for calm before you speak.** If something is bothering you, don't bring it up in the heat of the

moment. Wait until things are quiet. Choose your timing carefully—avoid late nights, empty stomachs, or moments of high stress. Emotional receptivity matters.

2. **Seek to understand their perspective.** You don't have to agree but try to see where your partner is coming from. Acknowledging their point of view can open up the conversation, even if you see things differently.

3. **Choose the relationship over the argument.** Ask yourself: what matters more—being right, or being close? If the relationship wins, then let it win. Set down the sword. Soften your stance.

4. **Don't expect your partner to fill every need.** If you're feeling neglected or unsupported, ask yourself: is this something they're truly capable of giving? And if not, how can you give it to yourself? Michelle Obama shared that when she was feeling resentful about always being the one to care for the kids while Barack prioritized his workouts, she thought marriage counseling would fix him. But what she learned instead was that *"It wasn't up to my husband to make me happy. I had to learn how to fill myself up and find the tools to nurture me."* [23] Sometimes the shift begins when we stop waiting for someone else to give us what we haven't learned to give ourselves.

5. **Notice when your ego is in the driver's seat.** Sometimes, the conflict isn't about the issue at hand—it's about protecting a wounded part of yourself. When something

---

23 *Michelle Obama, The Light We Carry (2022)*

hits a nerve, stop to consider. Is it really about them? Or is it something deeper in you asking to be healed?

6. **Strengthen your core so you don't need armor.** The more confident you become in your worth, the less you'll need to defend it. Vulnerability won't feel like weakness—it will feel like truth. And truth is powerful.

7. **Let the little things go.** Not every offhand comment deserves a response. Sometimes people say things they don't mean—especially when they're tired, frustrated, or stressed. Instead of reacting, zoom out. Ask: what else might be going on here?

8. **Stop replaying the argument in your head.** Ruminating only keeps the pain alive. If you catch yourself getting stuck in that loop, hit mute. Turn your attention elsewhere. Take a walk. Play music. Reclaim your peace.

9. **Anticipate the pattern—then choose presence.** If you already know a particular dynamic always leads to conflict—a recurring topic, a specific tone, a predictable reaction—don't walk in blindly. Pause beforehand. Breathe. Notice the tension rising and anchor yourself in the present moment. Instead of bracing for battle, soften. Choose awareness over autopilot. Sometimes, simply naming the pattern before it unfolds gives you the power to break it.

What I've found is that when you shift your own behavior, even subtly, others begin to shift in response. The person you thought would never change might start reflecting back the calm and compassion you now embody.

When you stand strong in who you are, and stop fueling the fires of conflict, your relationship finally has a chance to grow. Without the weeds, it can blossom into something deeply rooted, resilient, and full of grace.

I'd like to share some words from Ruth Bader Ginsburg, Associate Justice of the U.S. Supreme Court, when she was asked about the best advice she ever received—for both work and life. On her wedding day, her "savvy" mother-in-law offered her a simple but powerful piece of wisdom: "it helps sometimes to be a little deaf".

Justice Ginsburg later reflected:

> I have followed that advice assiduously, and not only at home through 56 years of a marital partnership nonpareil. I have employed it as well in every workplace, including the Supreme Court. When a thoughtless or unkind word is spoken, best tune out.[24]

It's a graceful reminder that selective hearing isn't denial—it's discernment. Sometimes, tuning out is not weakness. It's wisdom. Choosing not to react may be the strongest move of all. And it might just be the thing that saves your peace—and your partnership.

---

24 https://www.forbes.com/sites/markmurphy/2020/09/20/ruth-bader-ginsburg-delivered-the-best-career-advice-youll-ever-hear-in-just-one-sentence/#29f7bb04113f

Power to Let Go

Parental conflict doesn't just create tension between adults—it ripples through the entire home, affecting children in ways that can last a lifetime. Even in otherwise healthy relationships, unresolved arguments and power struggles can chip away at trust and emotional safety.

That's why rising above ego is one of the most powerful acts of maturity a parent can model. When you know who you are—when you've made peace with your imperfections and grounded yourself in self-belief—you no longer need to win every argument to feel validated. You stop looking to others to make you feel worthy. Your need to be right loosens its grip, and with it, the tension begins to dissolve. Criticism no longer pierces so deeply, because it no longer defines you.

Mothers, you hold a quiet but profound power: the power to lead with emotional maturity. When you let go of defensiveness and accept your partner's or your children's views without needing to control or correct them, you create space—for openness, for honesty, for everyone to feel safe just being themselves.

QUESTIONS TO JOURNAL

- When you're in conflict with someone you love, do you feel the need to prove you're right and they're wrong? Why? What's truly driving that need?
- After listening and acknowledging their perspective, try stating your own clearly—once. If they don't respond with the same openness, let them know you've said

what you needed to say, and stop engaging. What starts to happen when you do this consistently?

- Do you get defensive when someone criticizes you or says something hurtful? Are they touching a nerve—a vulnerability you're trying to protect?
- What happens when you admit a mistake or acknowledge your own insecurity? Do you feel relief? Strengthened or exposed?
- What shifts when you stop expecting your spouse or co-parent to always say or do the "right" thing? If you stop relying on them to make you feel better when you're sad, lonely, or tired—and start filling that gap yourself—how does your view of them change? Over time, how do they begin to respond differently to you?

> To practice the process of conflict resolution, we must completely abandon the goal of getting people to do what we want.
>
> —Marshall B. Rosenberg

CHAPTER 9

Faith in What Will Be

Disappointment Breeds Discouragement, Faith Offers Hope

We were surrounded by flashing lights, big hair, and sequined jackets. The crowd was electric, waving glowsticks and belting out lyrics to every George Michael hit. It was a tribute show, packed with die-hard fans reliving the magic. And there, in the middle of it all, was my husband—smiling good-naturedly, watching the crowd with quiet amusement, and clearly a bit out of place. A few men openly checked him out, which he took in stride. He wasn't there for the music—he could barely name a single song—but he was there for me. And that mattered.

The chorus of George Michael's *"Faith"* kept looping in my mind—an unexpected, yet strangely fitting, anthem for parenting. For years, my husband and I spent countless hours driving our younger son to basketball practice—five days a week, sometimes two hours round trip. Two of those days included private training sessions. He seemed committed. We were all in.

We didn't expect miracles. We just wanted progress—some visible sign that all the hard work was paying off. A few more minutes on the court. A few more baskets made. Something to tell us it was working.

But growth doesn't always announce itself. There were more off-days than shining ones. Just when we'd catch a glimpse of momentum, something would knock it off course. The inconsistency made it hard to stay hopeful—and even harder not to let that disappointment show.

As a parent, you try to be the steady hand. The encourager. The believer. But when effort doesn't equal reward, your faith starts to wobble. You wonder if your support is helping—or if you're just dragging your kid through a dream that might not be his to realize.

Staying Positive Against the Odds

At least once a week, I found myself in a heart-to-heart with my older son about his future. Was he really destined to become a great MMA fighter? From the outside, it was hard to picture.

My mental image of a champion fighter came mostly from *Rocky* or a documentary on Muhammad Ali: sprinting up stairs, dragging tires, shadowboxing at dawn. He trained, yes—but not every day. And to a mother watching closely, the path didn't seem urgent enough.

I've always believed in his potential. My only concern was whether he was doing enough to meet it. He was lucky, I thought—we weren't pushing him into some prescribed career or demanding he follow a traditional path. We supported his dream. All he had to do was do the work. I was concerned about his progress, and my fundamental message to him is reflected in this quote from Sarah Ban Breathnach, *New York Times* best-selling author:

> The world needs dreamers and the world needs doers. But above all, the world needs dreamers who do.[25]

But when I voiced those thoughts, he bristled. "I *am* doing the work," he would say. "You just don't see what I do." He wanted me to give him space—and more than that, *faith*. To believe in what he was building, even when I couldn't yet see the structure.

And faith is hard. Especially when you're unsure whether you're helping or enabling. Especially when you're trying so hard not to say the wrong thing—and yet, somehow, you still do.

I consider myself a naturally positive person. I look for the good in people and situations. But as a parent, I often felt like I was walking a tightrope—wanting to encourage my son to push harder without discouraging him in the process. At times, I ran out of creative ways to say, "Get a job," without it sounding like a judgment on who he was or what he was doing. I tried to inspire him, to motivate him, but my words were too often received as criticism.

---

25 http://www.sarahbanbreathnach.com

Then, in a moment of frustration, he'd make a biting comment to his younger brother about missing points in a basketball game—and I'd think, *Wait a second. You're calling me negative?*

Back then, we used to argue in circles. We'd both say things we half-meant and regret them later. But eventually, when emotions settled, our conversations would often take a turn—a softening, an insight. One night, he shared something I'll never forget: that the negative comments he'd heard over the years had caused him to grow a thick outer shell. He needed it, he said, to block out all the pain. He was working hard on the inside to build himself back up.

I told him I admired that. That it takes strength to turn wounds into wisdom. And I could see it—his resilience, his grit, the self-awareness blooming under the surface. As I said in the previous chapter, when you grow strong on the inside, you no longer need to fight to be seen. He was doing that work.

Still, it was painful to know that many of those wounds had come from inside our home. My husband and I wanted the very best for him, but we were operating out of fear. He had put all his eggs in one basket, and we couldn't see him carrying it. We worried the window of opportunity might close before he felt ready. And in our anxiety, we often delivered our concern as critique.

He told us he was learning from YouTube videos and educational podcasts. But we couldn't help thinking about all the doors he hadn't walked through, the skills he hadn't developed, the chances he'd turned down. We feared his dependence on us would harden into permanence—and we communicated those fears in ways that landed more like judgment than support.

And yet, there was plenty of praise too. We modeled hard work and self-belief and celebrated his talents. But somehow, he absorbed more of our doubts than our faith.

Eventually, we had to admit that our approach wasn't working. Our words weren't bringing him closer to independence or purpose—they were weighing him down. He felt our frustration like static in the air. He's sensitive, intuitive, and sharp—and he picked up on every unspoken fear.

In hindsight, I think we were doing exactly what Einstein warned against: "If you judge a fish by its ability to climb a tree, it will live its whole life believing it is stupid." We weren't seeing him for who he was. We were measuring him by what we feared he might never become.

That fear reminds me of a moment we shared years ago—one that became a lasting metaphor between us.

We were at a beach in Fort Lauderdale, splashing in the waves, when I heard my sister scream. It took me a moment to realize we were alone in the water. The people on the beach had fallen silent. Dozens of eyes were locked on the same spot—something in the water, right beside me. I looked down and saw a dark, blurry shape, five feet long, moving toward us. I panicked. Grabbing my son, I swam, kicked, stumbled towards the shore. But my swimming was clumsy, and I felt we weren't moving fast enough. So I put him down and told him to run to my sister, who had one arm outstretched while clutching my daughter in the other.

As he ran, I turned back, ready to face what I imagined was a shark. I pictured myself punching it in the nose, doing anything to protect my kids. But just as I turned, he ran back toward me and grabbed my leg. Terrified, I shook him off and shouted, "Go!" Then, with my heart pounding, I spun around ready to confront the threat—only to find the "shark" had disappeared.

Later, the lifeguard casually told us it was probably just a tarpon—large, fast, but harmless. We were relieved but shaken.

The incident became one of those family stories we often recounted—but with wildly different versions. In mine, I protected him before preparing to defend us both. In his, I kicked him off me to save myself. I tried to explain, to correct the record, but it didn't matter. His version had already taken root. Eventually, I stopped trying to argue.

Because here's what I've learned: his perception is his reality. And if he felt abandoned or hurt, that pain is real. No amount of explaining will undo it.

What I *can* do is apologize for the times I didn't get it right. I can affirm his worth. I can tell him again and again how loved he is. That he is special, talented, and unlike anyone else in the world. And I can provide positive reinforcement whenever I see him working towards his goals. These days, we don't always hug it out—but we'll share a fist bump, and sometimes, that's enough.

Overcoming Disappointment

One Sunday, as I sat in church listening to our pastor speak on *The Healing at the Pool* from the Gospel of John,[26] something

---

26 John 5:1-8 (KJV)

clicked. The story tells of a man who had been an invalid for thirty-eight years, lying beside a pool rumored to have healing powers. When Jesus asked him, "Do you want to be well?" the man didn't say yes. Instead, he gave a long explanation—about how no one would help him into the water, how others always got there first. He had grown so used to his struggle that he clung to it, even when healing was right in front of him.

It hit me: how much I had been doing the same. My husband and I had spent years stuck in frustration—worrying about our son, rehashing disappointments, feeling defeated by every setback. Like the man at the pool, we had become attached to our reasons, our fears, our need to explain why things weren't working.

And in the process, we were hurting not just ourselves—but our family.

The arguments, the tension, the hovering doubt—we didn't mean to, but we were dimming the light in our home. We needed a shift—not just in strategy, but in spirit. We needed to stop living in fear of what wasn't happening and start choosing faith in what *could* be.

Even when it felt like the evidence wasn't there. Even when we couldn't yet see the way forward.

After one especially difficult basketball losses, I overheard my younger son's coach tell the team, "When your parents give you a hard time, ignore them. Focus on the good things and learn from the bad." His words stung. Not because he was wrong, but because I recognized myself in them. **We were pushing our**

kids so hard that we didn't notice we were draining their desire to try.

It reminded me of another moment of collective disappointment—when millions of *Game of Thrones* fans, after years of investment, were let down by the final episode. Over a million people even signed a petition demanding a do-over.[27] They wanted a more satisfying conclusion, one that matched the epic journey that they had been on.

But the truth is: **it's not our story to write.**

And this applies profoundly to parenting too. We try to satisfy our cravings for something more spectacular that would light us on fire and cause us to jump from our chairs and scream, "Yes!" We may want a certain arc for our children's lives—a beautiful rise, a triumphant ending—but ultimately, their story is their own. Our job isn't to write it for them. It's to walk beside them, love them, and believe in them no matter how the plot unfolds.

We can choose to celebrate the journey—the growth, the little wins along the way—instead of measuring our children by what hasn't happened yet. Because some will walk, some will stumble, some will soar. But all deserve to feel deeply loved as they find their way.

Let's stop asking, "Why hasn't it happened yet?" or "Why don't they behave like that other kid?" Instead, let's ask: "How can I show them that they are enough?" Let's trade judgment for joy.

---

27 https://www.change.org/p/hbo-remake-game-of-thrones-season-8-with-competent-writers

Let's see them not for who we want them to be—but for who they already are.

Because they are wondrous. Brilliant. Divine.

And when we meet them with faith instead of fear, they rise.

Testing Times

Parenthood will test your faith—again and again. Especially when the path forward is uncertain, and the results don't seem to match the effort. These are the moments when you have to hold steady, keep your heart open, and believe that something better is making its way toward you... even if it's coming slowly.

My husband gave me a masterclass in this kind of faith during one of our toughest seasons.

We were in Las Vegas for the annual AAU basketball championships. It was our fourth trip to the tournament with our younger son, and by then, I knew what to expect. Each year, he was one of the last players off the bench. This time, his usual Division 2 team wasn't playing, so he joined the more elite Division 1 team for the experience. I didn't expect much playing time, but still, I hoped for a chance for him to show what he could do.

He got in during the early games, especially when his team was up by twenty points. He played well—smart and focused. But when the matchups got tougher, he stayed sidelined. Finally, in the last seven minutes of the quarterfinal, the coach called his name. This was it. I held my breath.

He stepped onto the court, facing players taller and stronger than him. As soon as he touched the ball, defenders swarmed him. They stripped it from his hands before he had time to find his rhythm. He hustled, he tried—but the scoreboard didn't reflect his heart.

I felt crushed. I had wanted so badly for this to be the moment he broke through.

I texted my husband a quick update—maybe a little deflated—and his reply came back with quiet strength: *"That's seven more minutes of experience. He's got work to do."*

That was it. No drama. No disappointment. Just faith.

His words helped me shift my own mindset. Instead of greeting our son with sadness or frustration, I greeted him with pride and encouragement. He had shown up. He had fought. And he had grown.

Sometimes, faith doesn't look like fireworks. It looks like seven quiet minutes on a hard court... and a father who still believes the best is yet to come.

Keeping the Faith

Disappointment and negativity no longer have a place in our family's vocabulary. That doesn't mean we're perfect—we still mess up, say the wrong things, and fall into old habits. But now, we catch ourselves. It starts with awareness—and a commitment to do better.

I imagine holding an umbrella over my family—not to shield us from the storm, but to shower us with belief. With encouragement. With a quiet but constant reminder that each of us is powerful and full of promise. That we are enough, just as we are—and that greatness already lives within us.

And I'm starting to see the difference.

My younger son, who once struggled with academics and basketball due to ADHD, has made remarkable progress. Instead of focusing on outcomes, we praise his persistence. He never lets challenges dim his spirit. His resilience, work ethic, and grit have transformed him. He earned school honors for perseverance and made the high school basketball team—something he once believed was out of reach. He was even put in as a difference maker, trusted by the coach more than once to shift the game's momentum—and he rose to the occasion each time.

Now, we watch his games with bated breath. When he sinks a three-pointer or drives to the hoop with bold determination, we erupt with pride—not just for the points, but for the journey that brought him there. Our faith in him has helped him believe in himself. And his confidence has lifted us all.

My older son is finding his stride too. He's now training regularly with a personal coach who's worked with UFC champions. Just recently, a haircut and shave gave him more than a new look—it gave him a fresh perspective. The journey continues, but as he always says, **"Everything begins with positive belief and faith."**

I used to wonder if that was true. But now, I see it everywhere. The more I choose to believe, the more things begin to shift. The energy in our home is lighter. Our hearts are fuller.

And I have started to believe it. That somehow, the stars will align, and each of my kids will end up achieving what they were put on this earth to do.

When It Don't Make Sense

At the 2025 BET Awards, gospel legend Kirk Franklin delivered a speech that left a strong impression. As he accepted the Ultimate Icon Award, he said: "What I really do don't make sense... that's when you know it's God. When it don't make sense."[28]

And he would know. Kirk Franklin grew up in poverty, abandoned by his parents, raised by a woman who collected aluminum cans to pay for his piano lessons. He never learned to read music formally. He has said openly, "I don't even know how to sing." And yet—he revolutionized gospel music, won twenty Grammys, and reached millions of hearts. His life is living proof that success, favor, and impact don't always follow a logical path. His message wasn't just about fame or talent. It was about divine timing. Grace. Possibility. It's about believing even when nothing adds up. Because sometimes, when things make the least sense, that's when something miraculous is unfolding.

---

28 https://youtu.be/4MjqBKBI8_M

Power to Trust What You Can't Yet See

We live in a world that worships achievement. From the moment our children are born, we imagine the dazzling futures they might have—doctor, entrepreneur, champion, genius. We paint visions of greatness and share them proudly with our loved ones. But somewhere along the way, those dreams can harden into expectations. And when our children struggle to meet them, they may feel inadequate, ashamed, or even resentful.

They might push harder than they should—or push back harder than we expect.

But here's the thing: our faith in them can't be tied to outcomes. It can't hinge on grades, trophies, or whether their path looks logical to anyone else. **The most powerful kind of faith is the kind that sees and celebrates who they are right now—not someday, not maybe, but today.**

Because real faith doesn't demand proof. It simply believes. It breathes life into potential... even when *it don't make sense.*

Our children may not always make sense to the world. They may not take the expected route. But that doesn't mean they're lost. It may just mean that something extraordinary is being written. And our job? Is to keep the faith.

So, moms—choose to meet your children where they are. See the spark in their eyes. Notice the small victories. Listen to the song in their voices. When we believe in who they are today, they begin to believe it too. That belief becomes fuel, lighting the way forward—even on paths we can't yet see.

QUESTIONS TO JOURNAL

- When your child doesn't meet your expectations, how do you typically respond—internally and outwardly?
- What emotions come up for you in moments of disappointment? Do your reactions move the relationship forward or create distance?
- Can you reframe disappointment as a signal to shift perspective? What could you say or do differently to build connection and encouragement?
- When you choose to focus on effort, growth, or your child's unique qualities instead of outcomes, what changes do you notice—in them and in yourself?

> Behind every child who believes in himself is a parent who believed in them first.
>
> —Matthew L. Jacobson

CHAPTER 10

Embracing Miracles
The Improbable Becomes Possible Once You Believe

The Bible recounts the many miracles performed by Jesus—turning water into wine, healing the sick, feeding thousands, walking on water, calming storms, and raising the dead. For centuries, these sacred stories weren't just tales of the past—they were reminders that the extraordinary could break into the everyday, that the divine could touch down in human lives. But somewhere along the way, we stopped expecting the miraculous.

Today, we've grown skeptical. Science explains away mysteries that once would have been labeled supernatural. We're too busy, too distracted, too grounded in logic to leave space for wonder. And yet—what if miracles haven't vanished? What if we've just stopped noticing them?

For some, miracles are still very real. In 2023, NFL player Damar Hamlin collapsed on the field after his heart stopped mid-game. Millions watched in shock as medics performed CPR for over ten minutes. What followed was a global outpouring of prayer—from fans, teammates, even sportscasters live on air. Against all odds, he woke up days later with no brain damage.

And in another headline-making story, a newborn baby in Syria was pulled from the rubble of a collapsed building after a devastating earthquake—alive, her umbilical cord still attached to her mother who didn't survive. Locals said they had prayed non-stop, believing that someone might still be alive beneath the ruins.

Then there was the Air India plane crash—nearly 250 lives lost, yet one man survived. His survival doesn't erase the sorrow. But I imagine, to him, it felt like divine mercy—an unexplainable thread of grace in a moment of unspeakable loss.

These stories may sound extraordinary—fit for news headlines or faith-based films. But what if miracles aren't rare, distant, or only for the chosen few? What if they're woven into our everyday lives, quietly unfolding around us, just waiting for us to pay attention—and believe?

Little Miracles

I hadn't given much thought to miracles until recently, when a remarkable event occurred. I almost want to call it "a miracle," though I know it probably doesn't fit the textbook definition—there's likely some scientific, albeit undiscovered, explanation for what occurred. Still, it meant something. It felt like God's quiet way of reminding me that miracles do happen—and that I should keep believing in the impossible.

But before that "miracle," there were smaller, more trivial moments that seemed to orbit around it. The kinds of coincidences we brush off, yet they send a strange tingle through your body. They reminded me of something Will Smith once said about the power to bend the universe to our will:

> That if we dream something, if we picture something, and we commit ourselves to it, that is a physical thrust towards realization that we can put into the universe… That we are going to bend the universe, and command, and demand that the universe become what we want it to be.[29]

It might sound minor, but I've tested that power a bit. I've always believed I can figure things out, fix what's broken, and find what's lost. People say I'm lucky—I rarely lose at poker, and somehow, in tricky situations, things tend to work out for me.

Whenever my kids lose something valuable, I always say not to give up—I'm usually convinced we will find it. And more often than not, it turns up. Like the day my daughter lost her retainers. We searched the whole house, top to bottom. No luck. She was panicking that her teeth were already shifting, and I was dreading the hundreds of dollars I would have to spend to replace that custom-molded piece of plastic.

Finally, I thought to text our house cleaner to see if she remembered seeing them. She replied that she had, and that she'd placed them in the plastic container next to my daughter's bed. So I rushed to check. My daughter gave me a look and said,

---

29 http://www.mindpowernews.com/BendTheUniverse.htm

"Really, Mom? You don't think I already checked there?" Still, I opened it—empty.

I messaged the cleaner again, and she insisted: *Plastic box by her bed.* I checked again. Still nothing. I opened drawers, cleared the table, even crawled under the bed. No retainers.

A few days later, our cleaner came by. She walked straight upstairs, opened that very same container—and there they were, sitting right inside.

You've got to be kidding me.

I couldn't believe it. We'd looked there at least three times. Could she have somehow slipped them back in? Not likely. This is someone we've trusted for years. We gave up trying to explain it and called it what it felt like: a tiny miracle. A mystery wrapped in convenience. And one that saved me hundreds of dollars—and my daughter's perfect smile.

The Impossible Made Possible

There was another mystery involving my daughter—one that unfolded on a stage in Las Vegas, and another, far more profound, that took place in a doctor's office. The mentalist show was strange and fascinating. The medical event, however, I now believe was a true miracle.

A couple of years ago, during a trip to Vegas, my daughter was randomly chosen to go on stage at mentalist Frederic da Silva's show. It began with him tossing a ball into the audience, which bounced from person to person. Whoever caught it was handed a numbered card—five in total. These were not pre-selected participants, just regular audience members.

Then he turned to my daughter, asked her to close her eyes, and instructed her to imagine a spinning wheel filled with numbers. When he said "stop," she was to picture the number it landed on and say it out loud. He repeated this seven times, and each time, she called out a number, which he wrote down on a board visible to all of us.

Finally, he asked the five audience members to read their numbers aloud. Incredibly, the sum of those five numbers matched exactly the seven-digit number my daughter had just imagined in her mind.

We were stunned.

Afterwards, I tried to figure it out. Did the numbers on the cards magically change, without people noticing, while they held them in their hands? Could he have whispered something to her? Sent subliminal cues? But he had been standing across the stage the whole time. She said she wasn't aware of anything unusual—if anything, she'd changed her mind a few times before saying each number aloud.

We never figured it out. But it left us with a lingering thought: *What if there's more going on in the world than we've been taught to see?*

And then came the real miracle.

Here's an excerpt from my daughter's college application essay written in response to the prompt: "Obstacles encountered that were fundamental to later success in life":

I will never forget October 3, 2015, the day that I first experienced loss of sight.

"This will all be over soon," I thought to myself as I walked down Hall 100 in the dark. "Ouch!" I screeched as the locker scraped my arm. "Get out of my way!" "Watch where you're going!" hollered my unsympathetic schoolmates. As I stumbled unseeing, I couldn't help but wonder if I was in the middle of a nightmare.

However, when I got to the Health Office, I quickly realized this was no dream. By the time my mom arrived, my sight was partially back. She was scared, though, and rushed me to the nearest ophthalmologist that she could find. I told the doctor about the sleepless nights I had been experiencing because of severe neck and back pain. She reassured me, saying, "Hon, you'll be just fine," as she began to examine my eyes. A few minutes later, she looked at me strangely, and with a trembling voice, said to my mom, "Take her to the ER immediately!" These six words heralded my journey into the unknown.

Eventually, doctors diagnosed my daughter with pseudotumor cerebri—a condition caused by fluid buildup in the brain that mimics the symptoms of a tumor. It leads to severe headaches, nerve pain, and, in some cases, permanent vision loss.

With medication, her symptoms improved. But they kept coming back. For more than a year, the cycle continued. Fearing this would become a lifelong battle, we flew across the country to consult with a specialist at Johns Hopkins.

The CT scan revealed an abnormality in her brain: an obstruction in one vein and a narrowing in another. The doctor explained to us that a potentially dangerous surgery was the only effective treatment.

Up until that moment, I had been holding on to the belief that this condition might just disappear. It had been easier to hope when no one could find a clear cause. But seeing the scan, hearing the diagnosis, facing the word *surgery*—something in me sank. My hope for a spontaneous cure started to fade. I began quietly planning when the best time might be to schedule the operation.

Meanwhile, our entire family prayed. My sister wrote my daughter's name on a card at church and asked the entire congregation to pray for her healing. My mother did the same. I prayed every night during my bath, asking for a cure.

My daughter, meanwhile, had placed her medication on top of the closet and declared she would never need it again. I was upset and told her she was out of her mind—that she needed to take the medicine exactly as the doctor instructed. But she just looked at me calmly and said she didn't need it. And despite my protests, she did what she wanted.

Several months later, we returned to our local pediatric ophthalmologist. I had mailed him the CT scan in advance. When we arrived, he greeted us warmly and said, "The CT scan revealed very interesting results—but not in the way you might expect."

Before explaining, he examined my daughter's eyes. He noticed a slight swelling in the right one, which he said was likely a residual scar that might fade in time. Her left eye, however, was perfectly healthy.

Then he said something I will never forget.

"I reviewed the CT scan in detail and consulted with two other specialists, including a neurologist. We all came to the same conclusion: *Your daughter's brain is completely normal. There is absolutely nothing wrong.*"

I stared at him, trying to make sense of his words. *What? Had there been a mistake? A mix-up? Had the issue resolved on its own? Or had something unexplainable occurred—something beyond our understanding?*

Maybe it was a coincidence. Maybe I'm naive. Maybe I just want to believe. Maybe Johns Hopkins showed us someone else's brain. Maybe I missed a second container when looking for the retainer. Who knows?

But what I do know is this: there are moments in life that defy logic—and invite us to believe. Moments when prayers are answered, when the improbable becomes real, and when the ordinary cracks open just long enough for something extraordinary to shine through.

So why not choose to believe that miracles do, in fact, happen?

Why not look for them—*everywhere*?

Miracles in the Everyday?

Not all miracles arrive in hospitals or headlines. Some slip quietly into your life through timing, persistence, and a series of events so improbable, they feel orchestrated. That's exactly how we found our home.

I had been searching for nine months in the brutally competitive Bay Area housing market—where even modest homes can attract dozens of offers and go hundreds of thousands over asking. My must-haves included a view of San Francisco, which all but guaranteed I would be priced out. After so many disappointments, I had started to accept that what I was hoping for simply wasn't possible.

Then I saw a listing on Redfin that seemed too good to be true.

The open house was happening that weekend, but I was in Florida and couldn't attend. I asked my daughter to go, but she was terribly sick—barely out of bed—so I crossed it off the list, assuming it would slip away like so many others.

But she surprised me.

She rallied just enough strength to go, arriving late—after the open house had officially ended. As the listing agent walked toward his car, she caught him and asked if he would let her in.

He agreed. She took a video and sent it to me. From what I saw, it looked amazing. And she said they were accepting offers the day after I returned to California.

The moment I was back, I rushed to see it in person. The view took my breath away—an unobstructed panorama of the city and all the beautiful bridges, sparkling in the distance. We submitted a bid with an escalation clause that allowed us to go up to a maximum amount if needed to win, knowing it would likely go far above that. I warned my daughter not to get her hopes up.

She nodded. Calm. Confident. "I think it's going to be ours."

A few days later, we got the call—and just as I expected: we didn't get the house. I was disappointed. Deep down, I had been clinging to the hope that this was our way out of the small condo we had downsized into—the one where the neighbors always seemed to have something to complain about. I didn't want to spend the rest of our years boxed in like that. I wanted more space and peace. But once again, it seemed like that dream had slipped just out of reach.

I assumed my daughter would be upset too—but when I told her, she simply said "Okay," as if she already knew the story wasn't over.

And she was right.

The following week, our agent called with unexpected news: the original buyer had backed out. Were we still interested? We jumped at the chance, ready to go in at the higher end of our original range.

But then something even more surprising happened.

The listing agent told us to stick with the *lower* end of our bid for the sake of simplicity.

Later, when we discovered there were a few updates needed, we asked for an even greater reduction—just to see. It was a long shot. But the sellers agreed.

In the end, we got the house for $400K below what it was likely worth—something almost unheard of in the Bay Area market. Other agents were furious, calling our realtor nonstop and blaming the listing agent for not knowing the market. As it turned out, the owner had passed away (not in the home) and left the property to a charitable trust. There were no heirs. No emotional attachment. No appetite for negotiation. They just wanted it sold.

Somehow, everything had aligned in our favor: my daughter's last-minute visit, the timing of the buyer backing out, the unexpected price drop, and even a few bumps that smoothed themselves out. It was as if the universe had quietly cleared a path for us while we weren't looking.

Every evening, I sit on the deck, watching the sun melt into the bay, and I feel it again—that same quiet awe. Like maybe this view, this home, this life… is a miracle I get to live inside.

Visions of the Life Beyond

One Christmas, on a magical trip to Tahoe, we met a man on the train who felt like he'd stepped out of another realm.

The night before, my younger sister, brother-in-law, and I had stayed up late talking about religion and life after death. They're devoted Christians who attend church regularly and believe deeply in God's promises. We were planning a trip to Israel, hoping to visit the tomb of Jesus. I brought up a question they hadn't considered: What if no one really knows for sure where the tomb is? They had assumed it was historically verified, a matter of record. But I reminded them that something that happened thousands of years ago can't be confirmed with absolute certainty. I said, half-joking but half-wishing, "Wouldn't it be amazing if something happened to give us a sign? Something undeniable that could prove life after death."

The next morning, something curious happened—nothing definitive, but enough to make us wonder.

We boarded the Amtrak train to Truckee. On that scenic ride, you have to reserve a spot in the dining car, and we had booked a table for eight, as some in our group were still asleep or finishing a card game. Just as we sat down, one of the kids changed his mind and left. Because of the long waitlist, the waiter quickly filled the empty seat with a solo traveler.

The man had translucent skin, bright blue eyes, and a presence that felt almost electric. As we talked, he showed us photos of himself in the hospital after open-heart surgery. Then, with calm certainty, he told us that he had died—and returned.

He described passing through stages of the afterlife, including a place where he welcomed others as they crossed over. It didn't matter who they were, what they had done, or what they believed. Everyone, he said, went to the same place. There was only peace. No condemnation. No regret. His message was simple: *Don't take life so seriously. Be present. Learn, laugh, grow. That's what you're here for.*

After that, we jokingly—though not entirely—referred to him as the angel we met on the train. We can't prove he was telling the truth. But it was hard to ignore that he appeared the very next morning after we had asked for a sign.

I'm not saying it would take a miracle for all three of my children to achieve their dreams. But if it does, I choose to believe.

Because sometimes miracles don't come with thunderclaps or a voice from the heavens—but in the form of strangers on a train, a daughter moved by an unshakeable inner knowing, or a view so beautiful it silences your doubt. And once you begin to notice them, they're everywhere.

Power of Belief

Although I was raised Catholic and appreciated its rich traditions—including the awe-inspiring architecture of churches around the world—my understanding of God remained mostly intellectual. Over time, my curiosity about spirituality—and exposure to other faiths and philosophies—opened me to a deeper truth: that there may be a realm far beyond what we can see, touch, or explain.

As Hamlet said, "*There are more things in heaven and earth, Horatio, than are dreamt of in your philosophy.*"

You don't have to believe in miracles. But if you stay open to the possibility that a higher power is at work in this world, you may begin to experience life on an entirely different plane—one where the extraordinary brushes up against the everyday.

Moms, I invite you: don't shut the door on the improbable. Let your children dream boldly. Let them believe. And do the same for yourself. Stretch beyond what seems rational. Make room in your life for wonder—and watch the miraculous unfold.

QUESTIONS TO JOURNAL

- Do you believe in miracles? Is it possible that a hopeful outlook can actually bring about positive change?
- Close your eyes and imagine yourself living the life of your dreams. Maybe in this vision, your children are thriving, joyful, fulfilled. Hold that image for a moment. What do you feel in your body? Is there a spark, a warmth, a tingling—as if your cells have come alive?
- When you open yourself to possibilities beyond logic, do you notice a shift in how life feels?
- Ask your child to describe their vision for the future. Listen—not to critique, but to understand. Witness their imagination with respect.

> There are only two ways to live your life.
> One is as though nothing is a miracle.
> The other is as though everything is.
>
> —Albert Einstein

CHAPTER 11
Love in Everything
*Let Love Be the Power
Directing Your Light*

Bishop Michael Curry, the presiding bishop of the Episcopal Church, delivered a powerful sermon at a British royal wedding that captured global attention.

In it, he quoted the late Dr. Martin Luther King Jr., who declared:

> "We must discover the power of love, the redemptive power of love. And when we discover that, we will be able to make of this old world a new world. Love is the only way."

Curry went on to say:[30]

> "There's power in love. Do not underestimate it. Don't even over-sentimentalize it."

---

30 https://www.npr.org/sections/thetwo-way/2018/05/20/612798691/bishop-michael-currys-royal-wedding-sermon-full-text-of-the-power-of-love

Although I love and am surrounded by love, I couldn't honestly say I understood what either of them meant by the "power of love"—or that "love is the only way." Most parents love their children and would do anything for them, yet that love doesn't stop us from getting frustrated when they don't do what they're supposed to. We love our spouses and partners, but as I've shared earlier in this book, that love doesn't always prevent major disagreements or bridge the gap when communication breaks down or our priorities don't align.

In our day-to-day lives, we try to treat others with respect and do what's right—but I don't usually think of that as love. Most of the time, when I'm simply going about my routine, I find myself wondering, *what's love got to do with it*?

The Many Faces of Love

Love is one of the most powerful forces we experience. At its best, it uplifts, protects, and transforms. It's what binds parents to their children, friends across decades, and partners through seasons of change. Love gives us courage, helps us heal, and makes life deeply meaningful. But as powerful as it is, love is not always pure. It can be misunderstood, misused, or warped into something unrecognizable.

Love can wear many faces—some beautiful, some destructive. It may appear to be the source of jealousy and hate. Obsessive love can even turn dangerous. We've all heard stories in the news or seen movies where someone, consumed by betrayal, kills the very person they claimed to love. "If I can't have them, no one will," they rationalize. In these moments, love becomes a weapon, not a gift.

Conversely, at other times, love seems to lose its meaning entirely. It can even appear weak—used as a reason to stay in deeply unhealthy relationships. I know it's more complicated than it seems—why someone stays with a partner who abuses them physically or emotionally. But when "love" is cited as the reason, it's as if it's expected to override everything else, including safety, dignity, and self-worth.

Even in far less extreme circumstances, love can cause confusion and conflict when partners express it in different ways. According to Dr. Gary Chapman, author of *The Five Love Languages* [31], we tend to give and receive love through one or more of these five ways:

- Words of affirmation
- Acts of service
- Receiving gifts
- Quality time
- Physical touch

While it would be ideal to experience all five, for me, quality time and physical touch speak the loudest. I'd take a walk in the park, a cozy night at the movies, or a quiet weekend by the coast over a diamond bracelet any day. And even though my husband rarely says "I love you," the simple act of playing with my hair or kissing me goodnight is all I need to feel it.

---

[31] *The 5 Love Languages: The Secret to Love that Lasts* by Gary Chapman (Northfield Publishing, 1992)

His language is different. He equates love with acts of service and appreciates thoughtful gifts. Looking back, had we known about these differences earlier, we might have avoided some unnecessary conflict.

Acts of service, for me, don't come easily. As a mother of three with a full-time job in tech—and a husband who's not exactly quick to pitch in around the house—I don't have a lot of extra time, energy, or desire to take on more. I used to bristle when, on a rare free Sunday evening, he'd ask me to design a flyer or edit (which often meant completely rewrite) a business letter. My reluctance showed, and he interpreted it as a lack of support. For years, this created tension and misunderstanding between us. At times, I felt judged—not just for what I wasn't doing, but for who I was. Eventually, after many difficult conversations, he figured it out. He hired a temp to help with his business and began handling more of it himself.

Now, when I bring him tea or surprise him with breakfast in bed, he's visibly grateful. It doesn't have to be big. Even the smallest gesture, when it speaks the right language, can mean everything.

Ever-present Love

In a family, love isn't always loud or obvious. It often lingers just beneath the surface, disguised in the everyday, waiting to be noticed.

My kids used to think something was wrong with me because I didn't openly love our dog. I was the one who walked him, fed him, and cleaned up after him when he made a mess in the house. That, I would tell them, is a form of love. But they'd just shake their heads, baffled. Some days, I felt a flicker of affection towards him—like when he jumped off the couch and spun in circles the moment I put on my shoes and grabbed the leash. But other days, when it was raining or I had more pressing things to do, I just felt annoyed.

Something held me back from loving him the way my kids did. Maybe I never forgave him for nipping my daughter the day we brought him home. Maybe I was afraid to love him—still carrying the pain of losing my first puppy, Browser, whose healing I had once prayed for as a child. Or maybe I just saw him as one more responsibility in a life already overflowing with them. He was, as my kids said, "part of the family," a creature of God—but I couldn't force myself to love him.

That is, until he died.

Then I realized my love for him had been there all along—just buried beneath layers of obligation. The day before he passed, he barely moved and refused to eat or drink. I spent time with him, talking gently and stroking his soft, golden fur. He looked up at me, lapped up all his water, then walked outside to bask in the sun. He seemed peaceful. That night, he died in his sleep. I cried on and off for three days.

Love may also be temporarily forgotten or ignored. On the way home from celebrating Father's Day, my younger son leaned into me and started playing with my hair. My daughter, sitting in the back, commented that it was strange for a fourteen-year-old to act that way with his mom. My son replied that he was just showing affection. Even though he was leaning heavily on me and squishing me a little, I welcomed his love.

Noticing my mother-in-law on the other side of him, I encouraged him to give her a hug too. He leaned over, rested his head on her shoulder, and gave a half hug.

She sighed and said, "He's only doing this because you told him to. When he was younger, he used to love me. Now, he doesn't love me anymore."

My son smiled slightly but sat back up in the seat.

Grandma was feeling sorry for herself—as parents and grandparents sometimes do—when it seems all the love they've poured into the children isn't being returned. My son, who once spent weekends at her house being doted on and offered anything he wanted to eat (and oh, did he love to eat), at that time would barely call or visit. He resisted going over, mostly because they didn't have Wi-Fi.

It's a common phase as kids grow, where the free-flowing love of early childhood gives way to guarded distance. They become absorbed in their own lives, their image, their ambitions—and in doing so, lose touch with the simple joys and companionship of those who love them. But the love isn't gone. It's just tucked away, waiting for some moment of fear, loss or distance to bring it back to the surface—like a well about to burst. Years later, when my son saw his grandfather struggling to walk, his love rose up again—unmistakable and true. He became his caretaker, without being asked. He sat with him, brought him drinks, watched TV by his side. In those moments, I saw the depth of his heart. So much love, still very much intact.

Sometimes, love is there even when it's never said aloud. I don't remember hearing "I love you" much from my parents when I was a child. But I never doubted their love. I saw it in their attention, their sacrifices, their steady presence. I felt it in the warmth of their embrace.

Maybe because I've heard the words more often in TV shows—or because I once took a parenting class that encouraged us to say it daily—I say it to my kids all the time. I whisper it in my younger son's ear as I kiss him goodnight. I shout it through the closed bedroom doors of my older kids as they lay in bed. I don't say it because they need to hear it. I say it because I need them to know it's always there, whether spoken or not.

Love as a Means to an End

Tough love is often misunderstood. My older son accuses me of being a "hater" whenever I offer feedback about what I'd like to see more of in his life. What he doesn't understand is that love is at the heart of parenting. We put our children first and give, often without expecting anything in return. All we want is for them to be happy—living their best life, as their best self.

But in our effort to be 'good parents,' it's easy to slip into control mode—focused more on correcting, protecting, and preparing our kids than on loving them in a way they can actually feel. I look back at a particularly difficult season in my daughter's life. The deaths of three of her friends—each unexpected and tragic—shook her deeply. These weren't kids we knew. They didn't go to her school or live in our neighborhood. She had met them online and had been spending time with them in places far outside our safe little bubble. So when we heard about the first incident, we didn't ask how she was feeling. We panicked. We lectured her. We commanded her to stay away from certain people and places. But what we should have done first was simply listen, without judgment. We should have sat beside her, acknowledged her pain, and let her know she wasn't alone.

Sometimes, even with the best intentions, parents go too far. Like Denzel Washington's character in the film *Fences*.[32], who discourages his son's dream of becoming a football player. He spends most of the movie warning his son that the world will never allow a Black man to "rise above his station." Though his words are meant to protect, they come across as harsh and unloving. His son never recovers from the emotional distance. And Denzel's character never finds a way to say what's really behind the lectures: *I love you, and I'm scared the world will break you.*

I also read an article about a well-known actress who had a daughter with Down syndrome. With her first child, she believed her job as a mother was to prepare her child to succeed—physically, academically, socially, and economically. But when her second daughter was born, she was forced to reexamine that definition. This child would struggle just to keep up, let alone compete. In a moment of panic, she recalled:

> This simple voice came to me where I was like, "I don't

---

[32] https://en.wikipedia.org/wiki/Fences (film)

know what to do—oh, I'm supposed to keep her safe and I'm supposed to make her feel loved." And suddenly my understanding of my job as a mother completely distilled and opened.[33]

Sometimes, in the midst of confusion, we need to take off the authoritarian hat, kneel to our child's level, and simply offer love.

I remember when my daughter was about two or three years old and had a full-blown meltdown at an amusement park. Out of nowhere, she started screaming for ice cream—loudly and persistently. My mind immediately started racing: Should I give it to her? Should I say no and wait her out? Should I distract her? But something deeper broke through all that noise. I picked her up, looked into her eyes, and said, "I know you must be exhausted. Let's take a break." I held her tightly in my arms. She calmed down. In the end, she didn't even want the ice cream. What she needed was comfort. Connection. Love.

Instead of reacting with my own frustration, I let love take the lead. It broke through the chaos and guided me toward what she needed most in that moment. This, I've come to realize, is where love begins—not in perfection or control, but in presence.

Love is simple and straightforward. It cuts through the noise, dissolves confusion, and gives you clarity in the now.

---

33 https://www.yahoo.com/news/apos-grey-apos-anatomy-apos-134930795.html

The Spaciousness of Love

Love is constant. It knows the truth and leaves no room for doubt. It's the oak tree you can lean on when everything else feels unsteady.

Sometimes, even the strongest among us can falter—especially when they're under public pressure or facing harsh criticism. In those moments, it's not advice or solutions they need most. It's love. Unconditional, grounding love. Like a quiet anchor, it reminds you who you are when you've temporarily forgotten. It says, *lean here, we've got you.*

That kind of love has the power to restore confidence and bring someone back to themselves. It doesn't need to be loud or performative—it just needs to be real.

That's what love does. It binds a family together and becomes a wall against whatever forces threaten to tear it down. It softens the hard, dissolves the heavy, and transforms mountains into molehills. Love makes what once felt insurmountable suddenly feel small.

I saw this in my own marriage, too. In the chapter on conflict, I shared the difficult conversation—well, more of a one-way communication—where I told my husband I loved him, but we couldn't keep going on like that. I'd had enough of the tension, the moping, the passive-aggressive energy I sensed was tied to our struggles with our son. I braced for a defensive reaction. Instead, he was calm—almost relieved. Maybe it was the clarity of love I expressed that reassured him we'd be okay.

Later that week, we found our way back to each other. Since then, it feels like love has become our fuel. That conversation—hard as it was—turned into a moment of release. On that day, love became the cloud we could float on. It lifted us.

Of course, we'll need to refuel again. That's life. That's marriage. And that's when it helps to remember: **love is a choice**.

In the short film *The Mindset Behind Successful Relationships*,"[34], spiritual teacher Radhanath Swami compares two types of people to a honeybee and a fly. The honeybee searches for nectar, flitting from flower to flower—even in the midst of garbage, it stays focused on sweetness. The fly, by contrast, will do just the opposite. It will ignore an otherwise healthy person and "focus on sucking an infectious scab."

The lesson? Be the honeybee. Keep your attention on the goodness in others, even when flaws or frustrations threaten to take over. If we act like flies—constantly scanning for what's wrong—we'll miss the God-given gifts right in front of us. But when we choose to see the nectar, we strengthen our relationships and create space for love to flow freely.

Self-love

Love for oneself is paramount.

Like many people, I sometimes lack self-confidence and fall prey to the voices in my head that whisper, "You're not good

---

34 https://www.youtube.com/watch?v=rKSLjWvCa14

enough," "This isn't for you," "You don't belong," or "You're too lazy." But even in those moments of doubt, I know this much is true: I love myself.

Self-love doesn't mean thinking you're perfect. It means liking and respecting who you are, enjoying your own company, being honest about your strengths and weaknesses, and treating yourself with care. When you love yourself, you don't knowingly put yourself in harm's way—physically, mentally, or emotionally. You don't punish yourself. You nurture your body, your mind, and your spirit. You grow.

But love can't stop with the self. In a world increasingly shaped by division, hate, and fear, self-love must expand into something greater. Love must radiate outward.

Now, more than ever—at least from what I've seen—there is rising intolerance between people of different races, sexual orientations, religions, and political views. And yet, I still catch glimpses of hope. When I pick my kids up from school and see students of all colors and cultures laughing together, I feel proud of our community. I think of the motto from my country of birth: *"Out of Many, One People."*

Still, that ideal has been painfully tested.

Not long after Trump was elected president the first time, my children's high school was vandalized. Racial slurs were scrawled across the bathroom walls—not once, but on multiple occasions. One incident happened the day before my daughter's final exams. My children, who are of mixed race, showed no visible distress—but I was stunned. *How could this still be happening in the progressive California Bay Area, in this decade?*

It reminded me of a KQED radio interview I heard shortly after Obama's election. A member of the Ku Klux Klan, rather than mourning the rise of the first Black president, was jubilant—he believed the backlash would boost white supremacist recruitment. What should have marked the beginning of healing had instead unearthed a deeper, uglier resistance to change.

I felt something similar while watching the Notre Dame Cathedral burn. Though the fire wasn't racially motivated, the imagery stayed with me: this grand, sacred structure—built over 800 years ago, full of prayer and hope—reduced to smoke and ash. It felt symbolic of what was happening in our society. Destruction where there should be refuge.

At times, it seems like we're caught in a battle between the forces of good and evil. And we can no longer sit quietly on the sidelines watching the world unravel.

I've lived through incredible moments of progress—the end of apartheid, the fall of the Berlin Wall, the election of the first Black U.S. president, the legalization of same-sex marriage. It felt, for a while, like we were moving forward, dismantling walls that kept us apart. But lately, it seems we've begun building them again.

We grew up believing that good would triumph over evil, that doing the right thing would matter. And yet we've seen our ideals trampled by those who are louder, crueler, or more cunning. The people who play the game without conscience often seem to win.

But we are not powerless.

Movements like Black Lives Matter and Me Too ignited important moments of awakening. Many of us remember the global outcry after the murder of George Floyd—when people took to the streets demanding justice and dignity for all. And that call for conscience hasn't faded. Today, it echoes through protests against book bans and curriculum censorship, and in the new faces of student activism rising up on college campuses and in the streets. These are not just echoes from the past—they are living movements, urging us to act with clarity, courage, and love.

As with most things in life, progress isn't linear. For every two steps forward, we may take one step back. But we can't afford to be passive. As Bishop Michael Curry reminded us, echoing Dr. Martin Luther King Jr.:

> Darkness cannot drive out darkness; only light can do that.
> Hate cannot drive out hate; only love can do that.

I didn't fully grasp those words when I first heard them. But now, I'm beginning to understand. If we don't already possess that kind of love, we must grow it within ourselves.

With every small act of courage, compassion, and connection, we tap into love's immense power to transform—not just our own lives, but the lives of those around us.

Uncovering Love

You may not always notice the power of love in daily life. But in times of challenge—when life gets hard, messy, or uncertain—love has a way of revealing itself. If you're present enough, it can shine through the noise and illuminate the path ahead.

We saw this during the height of the global pandemic. Health workers, caregivers, and frontline employees took extraordinary risks—isolating from loved ones, showing up day after day, serving others at great personal cost. Why? Because of love. Not the sentimental kind, but a deep, quiet devotion to humanity. Even in darkness and despair, love propelled them forward. It was their fuel. Their force. Their light.

Love is what we're made of. It is our very essence. Limitless, abundant, and always available—whether we feel it in the moment or not. When we're tired, discouraged, or overwhelmed, we can tap into love and feel our strength return. Like magic, it can renew what's faded and reawaken what we thought was gone. When we love ourselves and love what we do, we radiate that love outward—and light the flame in someone else.

In the book, *The Synchronicity Key*,[35] David Wilcock writes about love's metaphysical power. Drawing on the "Law of One," he describes light as universal intelligence, and love as the force that molds and directs that light—creating tunnels of connection between life-forms. In simple terms, love is how we carry

---

35 *The Synchronicity Key* by David Wilcock (Dutton, Penguin Group, 2013)

light to each other. It's how we illuminate darkness or rekindle the light that's already and always there.

Now, I finally understand what Martin Luther King Jr. meant when he said:

> We must discover the power of love, the redemptive power of love. And when we discover that, we will be able to make of this old world a new world. Love is the only way.

Power of Love

I believe love is a progression that begins with self-love. When that foundation is missing, our relationships with others can become strained—tainted by dependency, or the unspoken expectation that someone else will reflect back to us what we haven't yet found within ourselves.

But when you're filled with love, it doesn't stay contained. It spills over. It uplifts those around you. It brings out the best in others. Love can become your power—your most effective way of making a difference in the world.

Moms, be mindful not to let your well-meaning efforts to protect and educate your children overpower or obscure the love that is always there. It's not enough to simply love them; they have to feel it. They need to recognize it—in your tone, your touch, your presence, your patience. They need to experience it in how you lead them, and how you let go.

QUESTIONS TO JOURNAL

- During interactions with your teenager, do you often find yourself trying to protect, correct, or control? You may be doing what you believe is best—but is your love and support clear in those moments? Is it expressed in a way they can truly feel?

- Are you like the fly that fixates on flaws, or the bee that seeks out sweetness? Can you see the goodness in others even when it's buried beneath layers?

- When you choose to lead with love, your problems may not disappear. But do they shrink?

- Is there a difficult situation you're facing right now, where love could transform the outcome?

- How could you use love to direct your light and create positive change—at home, at work, or in the world?

> *Love recognizes no barriers. It jumps hurdles, leaps fences, penetrates walls to arrive at its destination full of hope*
>
> —Maya Angelou

PART III

Launch and Discover Your Life Purpose

*No chance? Why the world is just eager
For things that you ought to create,
Its store of true wealth is still meager,
Its needs are incessant and great.*[36]

—BERTON BRALEY, OPPORTUNITY

---

36 https://dancingalone530.com/2018/06/16/opportunity-poem-by-berton-braley/

CHAPTER 12

Letting Go, Without Giving Up

Boundaries Protect You and Move Them Forward

It was a quiet Tuesday morning. The house was still, sunlight just beginning to spill through the windows. I held my steaming cup of coffee in both hands, savoring the warmth as I stood by the kitchen window, admiring the soft, golden view of the Bay. For a moment, everything felt serene—until my eyes landed on the mound of overflowing trash in the kitchen bin. Again.

The same sinking feeling returned. That small, peaceful window I had carved out for myself was now interrupted by the too-familiar sight of a task left undone—by everyone but me. Usually, I could count on my younger son to take care of it, but he was out of the house for the week, helping take care of his grandpa. Without him, the task had quietly fallen through the cracks. I'd already communicated—firmly and more than once—that I didn't want the responsibility of making sure it got done. I was already doing enough. But the trash lay there, untouched, as if daring me to act.

For a moment, I still heard the old voice in my head: *"Just take it out—it'll be easier."* Then I paused. That bag was no longer just trash—it was a signpost. A boundary. A choice.

Why This Matters— Especially for Women

That moment wasn't unique to me. It reflects a far-reaching pattern: **women carry invisible labor and emotional weight**. We say yes too often, manage too much, and prioritize caring for others at the expense of ourselves.

Research shows that this self-silencing isn't harmless—it harms women's health. A Times article connects suppressing our needs to serious issues like depression, anxiety—even heart disease and fatigue syndromes. Young women who stifle their voices are more likely to experience chronic fatigue, emotional distress, and psychosomatic illness.[37] Between the mental load of parenting, work performance expectations, relationship strain and creeping burnout, the pressure builds until something gives.

When Boundaries Become a Lifeline

I've spent years watching women confess:

---

37 https://time.com/6319549/silencing-women-sick-essay/

"I realized I needed boundaries when my energy vanished. Saying 'no' became the way I said 'yes' to myself."

These aren't just social media mantras—they're survival guides. One mother told me she started sitting in her car after family dinners—engine off, lights out—just to cry in peace and catch her breath. It was the only place she could be alone. That's when she knew: *something had to change.*

The Turning Point for Change

Before we can truly make a change, we have to acknowledge what we're holding. It's a weight many mothers carry in silence—managing the home, tending to the needs of the family and trying to guide our kids into adulthood while still being treated like the default caretaker. From taking out the garbage to setting limits with a struggling adult child, the thread running through it all, is *boundaries*. They can be difficult to hold, especially when love is involved—but they are also a vital expression of that love.

This chapter isn't a roadmap for launching your child. Instead, it's a call to protect your own heart while holding space for theirs. It's about the courage to say "enough" when love demands action.

When words no longer work, when enabling feels easier than holding firm, that's when love and courage intersect. It's time to draw the line—not out of anger or selfishness, but out of self-respect and hope.

From Launching to Living

I couldn't fix what held my son back—fear, his mental health, his bad choices and habits. And I know now that I'm not alone; 'failure to launch' is more common than ever. It doesn't mean we've failed as parents. In many cases, it reflects a mix of societal, economic, and emotional hurdles that today's young adults face.

One reason this pattern is so widespread today has to do with societal shifts in parenting norms. In our efforts to give our children more voice and empathy—often in response to our own upbringings—we may have swung the pendulum too far. Many of us became highly involved, highly invested parents. We helped with homework, managed emotions, and tried to smooth the way. Combine that with skyrocketing anxiety rates, a hyper-competitive world, and the escape offered by digital devices, and you have a generation with soaring expectations and fragile confidence.

In schools, children are given more power than ever before by teachers afraid to tell them "no" for fear of repercussions by parents, school administration, or the law—a stark contrast to the stricter school upbringing of earlier generations. Kids today are emboldened to resist authority and do or say whatever is on their mind. You only have to watch the many television shows targeted at tweens and teens to see how the media has also been complicit in handing more power over to our children by portraying adults as incompetent and kids like the ones with all the answers.

Teens and young adults are living much of their lives online—playing games, scrolling social media, immersed in entertainment. It's a powerful form of distraction, often more appealing than the effort real life demands. And while technology can offer connection and creativity, it can also delay maturity, obscure purpose, and make real-world responsibilities feel avoidable. Constant exposure to curated, filtered lives can foster unrealistic expectations, social comparison, and the feeling of never being enough. Online interactions, while abundant, often lack the depth and accountability of real-life relationships—leading to more loneliness, less resilience, and, in some cases, outright social withdrawal or cyberbullying.[38]

Recognizing the weight of these influences helped me release some of the guilt I felt about drawing a firm line. **The problem wasn't just parenting—it was the culture our kids are growing up in.**

That understanding didn't make the situation any less painful, but it did help me shift my focus—from trying to rescue him to reclaiming myself. Because while I couldn't control his path, I could take control of mine.

That choice—to hold the line with love—is the hardest one I've made. Yet, it became the most freeing, for my son and for myself.

---

38 Twenge, J. M. *iGen: Why Today's Super-Connected Kids Are Growing Up Less Rebellious, More Tolerant, Less Happy--and Completely Unprepared for Adulthood*, Atria Books, 2017.

The Delicate Balance of Parenting

Parenting today requires both courage and restraint. We must be steady in a world that feels increasingly unstable and resist the pressure to control every aspect of our children's lives. It's a delicate dance—being involved, but not overbearing; supportive, but not enabling.

We've heard the warnings: Helicopter parents[39] who hover and monitor every move raise kids who are less resilient, less willing to take risks, and more likely to panic when faced with real-life struggles. Then there are the bulldozer or snowplow parents, who clear every obstacle from their child's path. These children grow up ill-equipped to handle failure, advocate for themselves, or navigate life's inevitable setbacks.

Looking back, I can see how I leaned into bulldozer territory with my older son—questioning a teacher's communication when my son missed a deadline or did poorly in class or rushing to bring his trumpet to school when he forgot it. My intelligent, gifted, and creative son has not failed to launch—he just hasn't launched yet. It wasn't one decision or event that led us here; it was a complex mix of circumstances. ADHD may play a role, but I know he can thrive in the right environment. I also know there are things I could have done differently. Had I consistently allowed him to face the natural consequences of his choices—

---

[39] In 1990, child development researchers Foster Cline and Jim Fay coined the term "helicopter parent" to refer to a parent who hovers over a child in a way that runs counter to the parent's responsibility to raise a child to independence.

as I urge in Chapter 2—he may have better internalized the link between effort and outcome.

Hindsight gave me the clarity to create the acronym **FREE** in Chapter 3:

Foster a spirit of cooperation and giving back, establish Routine chores, teach children to Earn not receive, and Expect more.

When these principles are anchored in faith and love, they help raise children who are not only self-reliant but compassionate.

The past isn't a place for regret—it's a teacher. And I've learned. I've grown. And now I'm ready to help others who may be facing similar struggles.

That's why I created a second framework—CCBCC—for the stage when words no longer reach your child, when it's too late to begin practicing FREE, and what's needed is a reset.

CCBCC
Currency. Contract. Buttons. Commitment. Coaching.

But before we dive into the tools, I want to pause and acknowledge where you might be right now.

Maybe, like me, you've tried everything—reasoning, incentives, consequences, heartfelt talks. You've begged, bargained, and set deadlines that came and went. You're exhausted from caring so deeply and yet seeing so little change. You may feel stuck watching your child float in limbo, convinced of their own greatness but seemingly unwilling or unable to take the necessary steps toward it.

Maybe your child, like mine, proclaims with conviction, "I'm the greatest," echoing Muhammad Ali. They speak with charisma and vision, but when you offer help turning that vision into a tangible plan—with steps, deadlines, and check-ins—they recoil. They accuse you of nagging, of doubting them, of not understanding. Maybe they even say: *You've never achieved greatness yourself, so how can you guide me to it?*

Their words might sting—but they don't destroy you. Because you're no longer in the same place you once were. You've done the work. You've grown strong. You've developed the kind of strength that doesn't flinch—even when your child tries to shake you.

Still, your child has leaned on you for so long that they've forgotten how to stand on their own. In trying to support, you may have inadvertently enabled. And now they don't know where their strength ends and yours begins.

This is where **CCBCC** comes in—not as a punishment, but as a loving, structured boundary reset. A shift in the power dynamic that offers your child the opportunity to rise without you carrying them.

Let's break it down:

C — Currency

What does your child value most? It might be money, access to a car, phone privileges, or a roof over their head. This is their **currency**. If words haven't worked, leverage currency to create conditions for change. Not as manipulation, but as motivation. If they want adult freedom, they must also accept adult responsibility.

When I consulted with Parenting Modern Teens,[40] one of the first things they asked was, "What is your son's currency?" For him, it was money, car access, an iPhone, food, and a place to live. When they asked which of those things he was responsible for earning, I realized—I had given him almost all of it. No wonder he felt comfortable staying stuck. That's when we started drafting a contract. They warned me: with older teens and young adults, the patterns run deeper, and resistance can be strong. But if you want real change, you have to begin with absolute clarity—about what's expected, what will change, and what you're no longer willing to enable.

C — Contract

Set clear expectations. Don't just hope for change—write it down. A contract should outline exactly what your child is responsible for and what will happen if they don't follow through.

Defined actions might include:

---

40 https://www.parentingmodernteens.com

- Applying to at least three jobs each week until they find employment
- Attending therapy every Monday
- Taking out garbage and cooking dinner for the family once a week
- Paying rent (giving them time to get a job)

Consequences could be:

- Loss of car access, if they are still borrowing yours
- Limiting internet use or discontinuing financial support for their phone or car insurance bills
- A deadline to move out if agreed conditions aren't met

Be specific. When expectations are vague, disappointment and conflict are almost guaranteed. Clarity doesn't eliminate conflict—but it does reduce confusion, minimize power struggles, and create a shared understanding of what's expected and what happens next.

B — Buttons

You know your child's triggers—and they know yours. Be aware of the buttons they press to derail the conversation: guilt, blame, emotional outbursts, silence. Your job is to stay grounded. If they throw a tantrum, don't match it. If they call you a failure, don't spiral. Recognize their reactions as part of the old dance you're no longer performing.

In a recent meeting, I found myself advising another parent: "You have to be ready to hear your child say, 'I hate you.'" I said it not to frighten, but to prepare. When you draw clear boundaries, especially ones that challenge their comfort, you may provoke anger or rejection. That's not a sign you've done something wrong—it's a sign you've disrupted the pattern. Be strong enough inside to stand your ground. Know that holding firm is not harshness—it's love with a spine.

Hold the line.

C — Commitment

Once you set the contract, **commit** to it. Don't waiver. Don't negotiate every few days. Don't rush in to rescue them when discomfort hits. Growth requires discomfort. If they miss rent, don't waive it, have them work it off with tasks or responsibilities around the house. If they lose access to the car, let it happen. Discomfort can be a powerful motivator. When something matters, they'll work to earn it back. This is where your strength as a parent is tested. Compassion doesn't always look like comfort— it often looks like resolve.

C — Coaching

Instead of constant correcting or lecturing, shift into **coaching** mode. Listen more. Ask powerful questions like, "What do you want your life to look like a year from now?" or "What would taking one small step today look like?" You're not managing their life—you're helping them take ownership of it. Coaching invites growth without creating dependence.

My son once painted a grand vision—one so compelling it pulled me right in. Then came the list of things he needed to make it real: a haircut, a white shirt, gas money, a gym membership, personal training for his first amateur fight. I believed in him—so I funded it. But eventually, I realized: **if he truly believed in his dream, he'd find a way to invest in it himself.** That's when I shut down the "Bank of Mommy" and invited him to take ownership.

Coaching isn't about fueling inspiring promises—it's about holding space for action. Sometimes the most powerful thing we can do is step back and let reality speak louder than our support ever could.

Boundaries Aren't Just for Kids

Boundaries don't just apply to children who haven't yet launched. They are often essential in relationships, especially partnerships.

After trying several times to explain how draining it was to come downstairs to an overflowing garbage can, I realized that words weren't getting through. I had already shared how it disrupted my peace and added to a mental load I was already carrying. But nothing changed. So I set a clear, respectful boundary: If the garbage wasn't handled—without me having to remind anyone or take it out myself—I would no longer be responsible for laundry that wasn't mine.

It wasn't about being punitive. It was about rebalancing the invisible workload and preserving my peace. At first, it wasn't received well—but after a bit of reflection, my husband made sure one of our sons took responsibility. Not just as a one-time fix, but as a consistent pattern.

Not because I nagged or exploded, but because I held a boundary and followed through. That moment reminded me again: calm, consistent boundaries often speak louder than any plea. Not just with our children, but with the adults in our lives too.

Avoiding Drastic Action

Hopefully, you'll never have to take extreme measures—but sometimes, a firm boundary is exactly what's needed to spark change. For us, the turning point came down to one thing: money.

We had to seal every leak. I stopped giving my older son money for gas and MMA training for over a year, and eventually, he stopped asking. We asked extended family to offer only what he truly needed—gift cards or essentials—instead of cash for birthdays or holidays. Finally, his dad stopped employing him at his sports camps, where the blurred lines of family and business allowed him to work only when convenient.

It was vital for him to find employment where he was treated like an employee—not a son.

And that's exactly what happened. Running out of money pushed him to get his first real outside job, working for the Parks and Recreation department of a nearby city. The need for currency to fund his goals finally got him out of the house and into the workforce.

Then came the pandemic. Lockdown sent him right back.

When the cloud clears, we may have to start again. But something has changed. My son now has a clearer understanding of what it means to be an adult—and the boundary between support and enablement is no longer blurry.

If necessity isn't the mother of invention, it's at least a very persuasive motivator.

Power to Launch

In the previous chapter, I shared how essential it is for kids to feel loved. But love alone isn't always enough. True love, in these situations, must be coupled with strength.

Moms, I know the temptation to give in—especially when they wear you down. But giving in doesn't bring peace; it builds patterns of entitlement that are harder to undo later.

If you want your child to grow, *you* have to grow stronger. **Hold your line. Say what you mean. Follow through.**

And at the same time—respect their space. Don't micromanage or invade. Let them have ownership over their own lives. You cannot control the choices they make, but you absolutely have the right to protect what belongs to you: your time, your energy, your home.

When it's clear what's yours and what's theirs, only then are they ready to truly launch.

QUESTIONS TO JOURNAL

- Do you have a child who is struggling to launch? What is holding you back from taking steps to protect your boundaries and respect theirs?
- Are there forms of "currency" you're still providing that might be unintentionally enabling?
- How can you begin the shift from managing your child's life to coaching them towards ownership?
- Where in your home or relationships are unspoken expectations pointing to a need for clearer boundaries?
- What boundary are you ready to hold—and how will you communicate and reinforce it with clarity and love?

> You can't go back and change the beginning, but you can start where you are and change the ending.
>
> —C. S. Lewis

CHAPTER 13

Uncovering Purpose
The World Will Embrace You When You Know Who You Are

I lost my job at the end of last year. It wasn't dramatic—it was defining. I wasn't engaged anymore—not because I had lost interest in the work itself, but because I could no longer align with the company's direction or lack of clear purpose. Eventually, I told my manager that if she ever felt it was time to make a change, I would understand. A month later, just when I thought it might blow over, a one-on-one meeting appeared on my calendar. When the VP of HR joined the call, I knew exactly what was about to happen. The CEO had apparently come to a similar realization: that my interests and energy were no longer aligned with where he wanted to take the company. He gave me two months to prepare my team and search for my next role.

I wish I could say it was conscience that drove me to that moment, but the truth is simpler: I could no longer pretend. I had checked out—and it was becoming harder to hide.

Moving On

I can't thrive in a place where purpose is missing, and strategy is just a smokescreen. The company I worked for had become that kind of place. The CEO—its sole owner—was guided by something none of us could figure out. It wasn't customer value, market opportunity, or even employee engagement. We were pawns in a private game designed solely for his amusement.

Truth matters to me. And I can only perform for so long before the act becomes unbearable. So even though I was suddenly without income, it was time to go.

The obvious next step? Find another job in the same industry I'd been in for twenty-five years. But that idea filled me with dread. To me, it felt like choosing the blue pill in The Matrix—the illusion of security, the simulation we're trained to accept. It's the version of life where you play by the rules, stay in your lane, and trade authenticity for a steady paycheck.

The red pill, on the other hand, is reality. It's unpredictable and unfiltered—but it's also real. It's a life filled with passion, purpose, and truth.

For my generation, the red pill was rarely offered. Those who found it did so by chance or rebellion. And even when younger generations came along and showed us what it looked like to follow passion, we hesitated. We feared the unknown. We clung to duty and sacrifice, believing we had to endure so our children could be free.

But secretly, many of us are watching and waiting, hoping they succeed. Hoping they illuminate the way.

Choosing the Blue Pill

Still, I kept swallowing the blue pill. It made me sick at first—physically, emotionally. But then came the high: money, prestige, comfort. That's why, when a recruiter from Google reached out, I took the call. Her message was filled with enthusiasm: "The hiring manager is VERY EXCITED about your background! You'd be a GREAT fit!"

I was skeptical, but curious. I agreed to the interview.

After our conversation, the hiring manager told me he thought I was perfect for the role—but that we still had to go through the standard process. As part of the follow-up: I'd be evaluated on "Googleyness" and asked to solve questions like, "Design an alarm clock for the visually impaired," or "Estimate how many vacuums are sold in the U.S. each year."

My gut reaction: I'm too old for this. But it wasn't really about age. Before I declined, I had to ask myself a hard question: Am I walking away out of clarity or fear?

Unlike my children, who pursue dreams with no fear of consequence, I have responsibilities. Bills. Real-life concerns. My husband often shares the Parable of the Flood with our son—usually when he's passing up opportunity after opportunity, always searching for the perfect one. This time, I thought of it and wondered—was I doing the same thing? Was I passing up an opportunity that was right in front of me, just because it didn't look the way I expected?

> A man was stranded on his rooftop during a flood. He prayed for God to save him.
>
> Soon a rowboat came. "Jump in, I can save you!" the rescuer said. "No, thank you. God will save me," the man replied.
>
> Then a motorboat came. Same response.
>
> Then a helicopter came. Still, the man refused.
>
> Eventually, the man drowned. When he reached Heaven, he asked, "God, why didn't you save me?"
>
> God replied, "I sent you a rowboat, a motorboat, and a helicopter. What more did you want?"

Sometimes, opportunities come as lifelines, even if they don't look like what we imagined. Other times, they're just distractions from the deeper work of discovering what we actually want.

I went through with the follow up step. From the start, I knew it wasn't going to work. The interviewer's voice was muffled, I couldn't hear him well, and the whole thing felt off. But I stuck with it until the end.

That interview confirmed what I had suspected: this wasn't for me. I wasn't afraid of the challenge. I just no longer wanted to mold myself to fit into someone else's machine.

I needed to learn to say no. Not to others—but to the part of myself that still chased external approval. The part that confused comfort with purpose.

Passion in Work

The truth is, I've been at war with myself for years. Torn between what I think I should do and what I genuinely want.

But as Terry Orlick once said:

> The heart of human excellence often begins to beat when you discover a pursuit that absorbs you, frees you, challenges you, or gives you a sense of meaning, joy, or passion.

I felt that pulse at an Usher concert I attended with my daughter. In the middle of the show, Usher paused to take in the crowd. The joy on his face was undeniable. *That's it,* I thought. That's what it looks like when you are doing the thing you were born to do.

I've seen a similar look before—on my daughter's face after she performed in *Twelve Angry Men* and received a standing ovation, on my son's face when he made the basketball team, on my husband's face when our older son won his first martial arts gold medal.

I don't want my children to drag themselves through a career. I hope they will be propelled by something powerful and internal—an energy that comes from knowing who they are and what they're meant to do.

The people I most admire weren't chasing money. They were listening to something deeper—the inner voice that told them who they were and what they were meant to do. And when you listen to that voice, it leaves clues—signs that you're on the right path.

Discovering Ikigai

In my search for purpose, I discovered the Japanese concept of *Ikigai*—your "reason for being."

It's often visualized as a Venn diagram, sitting at the intersection of four key elements:

- What you love (passion)
- What the world needs (mission)
- What you're good at (vocation)
- What you can get paid for (profession)

When these align, you don't just make a living—you come alive. If you can find your Ikigai, it is said, you will achieve fulfillment, happiness and will live a longer life.

For over two decades, I had a good career. But I always watched the clock. The joy was real, but it was limited.

If I dissected my job in product management, it came down to two things: driving product success and developing people. The industry valued the first; my heart was in the second.

Reigniting the Flame

I wish I had a burning passion pulling me forward right now. But sometimes, I draw a blank. That fire I had at seventeen—when I spent a summer studying for the SATs, aiming for MIT—feels extinguished. I can't find the pilot light.

Maybe it's buried beneath years of rules, conditioning, and compromises.

In *The Seven Spiritual Laws of Success*[41], Deepak Chopra explains:

"The only source of wealth and abundance is the Self... When you chase money, you exchange your true Self for symbols of your Self."

That's exactly what I've been doing. Searching for financial freedom so I can one day do what I want. But in the process, I lost sight of what makes me me.

Chopra also writes that the search for security is an illusion. If we stay attached to it, we stagnate. We stop evolving.

---

41 *The Seven Spiritual Laws of Success* by Deepak Chopra (New World Library, 1994).

I don't want to decay in the comfort of a false sense of safety. It's time to shed the armor I've built, reconnect with the voice within, and listen for the whisper of God.

As Pope Francis once said:

"Vocations aren't the result of planning, but an encounter with God that changes your life."

The Questions to Ask

The journey to discover my life purpose continues, but along the way, I've learned the essential questions we all need to ask ourselves:

What am I curious about?
Steve Jobs once told the Stanford graduating class, "You cannot connect the dots looking forward; you can only connect them looking backward." In other words, follow your curiosity even if you don't yet know where it will lead—it may be guiding you toward your destiny.

Children are naturally curious. But over time, adults grow tired of their questions, and society teaches them to stop asking. We become cynical or close-minded and forget the joy of discovering something new. But curiosity is a form of aliveness. What fascinates you? What draws you in and makes you forget to check your phone? When you're deeply curious, your senses sharpen—and you step closer to your true path.

What lights me up inside?
After a sleepless night of travel, I can arrive in Kingston for a family reunion and stay up another full night talking and laughing. That's the feeling of being deeply energized—to be fueled by joy, not just caffeine. But how do we hold onto that feeling in everyday life?

Start by releasing the expectations about what *should* make you happy. Let yourself notice what actually does. Pay attention to strong emotions—even the painful ones. They might be pointing to something that needs to shift. What gives you energy, even when you're tired? What drains you, even when you're rested? Who lifts you up just by being around? These are clues.

Philosopher and civil rights leader Howard W. Thurman said, *"Don't ask yourself what the world needs. Ask yourself what makes you come alive, and go do that, because what the world needs is people who have come alive."*

What absorbs me and makes me lose all sense of time?
Have you ever been so immersed in something that you forgot to eat? Or looked up from a project to realize hours had flown by? These are flow states, and they're golden.

Whether it's building, creating, teaching, speaking, researching, connecting, or helping—whatever draws you in and makes time vanish is worth noting. Find ways to do more of that. As Richard Branson said: *"Have fun, work hard and money will come. Don't waste time—grab your chances."*

What brings out the best version of me?
When you're aligned with your purpose, something changes.

You show up fuller, clearer, more powerful. Your best self begins to emerge—not from ego, but from truth.

It doesn't matter if your path is traditional or unconventional, public or quiet. When you are connected to what lights you up, your presence uplifts others. As Pope Francis said: *"We are all born to help each other. No matter how difficult it is… Life is good when you are happy; but much better when others are happy because of you."*

What allows me to be authentically myself?
Trying to be someone you're not is exhausting—and unnecessary. If you don't recognize the unique value you bring, the world won't either.

We all have a natural zone of brilliance. But it gets buried under years of conditioning. To rediscover it, think like a toddler learning to walk—unashamed, persistent, curious. Meryl Streep put it best: *"The formula of happiness and success is just being actually yourself, in the most vivid possible way you can."*

Once you begin answering these questions honestly, you can follow your path, as I'm learning to do. Choose the one thing you'd do if you knew you wouldn't fail. Trust that if it's meant to be, it will be. And when the signs and connections appear, you'll know you're on the right track.

Feel your heart burst with the joy of living on purpose. Don't forget—you're not alone. As Rumi said:

What you seek is also seeking you.
You don't need to hustle for worthiness. You were born with it. The moment you stop apologizing for who you are and start showing up as yourself, the universe shifts.

Power to Be You

It's time to stop cowering to bosses, spouses, or societal expectations. We're not perfect—no one is. But we are powerful, gifted human beings with something meaningful to offer.

Your dream job isn't looking for someone you're pretending to be. It's waiting for you.

When you step into your power, your energy connects with the vibrance of the universe—and the world will rise to meet you.

At the time I wrote this chapter, I had decided to stop waiting for permission and start building something of my own. I committed to publishing this book and launching a coaching practice to help others tap into their own power. If you're reading this, and it wasn't through a promotion or a personal connection, then I must have made a breakthrough. And that means you can too. If it's possible for me, it's possible for you. You just have to commit to making it happen.

QUESTIONS TO JOURNAL

- When you go to work, does your authentic self shine through?
- What steps can you take to recognize or remind yourself of your unique talent and strengths?
- Are you propelled by passion in your work? How can you reintroduce energy into your career?
- How will your world change when you do?
- What whispers have you been ignoring? What has your inner voice been trying to tell you?

> There is no passion to be found playing small—in settling for a life that is less than the one you are capable of living.
>
> —Nelson Mandela

CONCLUSION

Strengthen Your Core, the Rest Will Follow

In *The Lesson of the Butterfly*, Paulo Coelho,[42] tells the story of a man who watches a butterfly struggle to emerge from its cocoon. Wanting to help, he gently assists the butterfly in breaking free. But despite his kind intentions, the butterfly remains grounded; it cannot fly.

What the man failed to realize was this: the cocoon's resistance—and the butterfly's effort to push through it—were essential. That struggle was nature's way of strengthening its wings. Without it, the butterfly was not ready to take flight.

Over the past few years, I've lived my own version of that metamorphosis. Thirteen hard-earned lessons have reshaped how I see myself, my children, and the purpose of motherhood itself. These lessons did not come easily. They came through resistance, heartbreak, failure, faith, and growth.

---

42 http://paulocoelhoblog.com/2007/12/10/the-lesson-of-the-butterfly/

And each of them points to a deeper truth:

The power to create change begins not in others, but within ourselves.

Once you understand that, you begin to live differently. You parent differently. You lead with more purpose, and less fear.

These are the principles I now hold close:

- Loosen the reins, so they can discover their own path.
- If you knock down every hurdle, they'll never learn to jump.
- Teach them to fish, then step away from the shore.
- Control your mind before it takes control of you.
- Don't shrink your dreams to fit someone else's fears.
- Inner power is stronger than willpower.
- When you let go of being right, you begin to see more clearly.
- If you're strong on the inside, there's no need to fight.
- Disappointment breeds discouragement; faith offers hope.
- The improbable becomes possible once you believe.
- Let love be the power directing your light.
- Boundaries protect you and move them forward.
- The world will embrace you when you know who you are.

I don't claim to live these lessons perfectly. I still stumble, still forget, still get pulled off course. But that's part of the path too.

The important thing is that I now have a compass—guiding truths that help me find my way back. These values have become my North Star. When I stray, I don't feel lost. I know which direction to turn.

This work isn't easy. Growth rarely is.

But it's the struggle that makes you strong. And as hard as it may be to accept, the lesson of the butterfly still holds true.

Learning to Transform

My daughter recently emerged from her own cocoon during her first year away at college. Though she was studying what she loved, she found herself surrounded by people who drained her energy—roommates who called themselves witches, classmates who used her for clout, and moments that tested her spirit. She fell into a dark space for a while, questioning others and herself.

But she didn't stay there.

She meditated. Reflected. Released what wasn't hers to carry. And she rose, softer and stronger. Her light returned even brighter. Watching her talk to her brother about breaking cycles, facing inner demons, and choosing growth over escape, I realized: in her own words, she was claiming a legacy—one that would break patterns instead of repeating them.

She shared her experience with her older brother, explaining why she felt ready to move on to the next phase of her life. She urged him to reflect, meditate, journal—*do something*—to interrupt the cycle he'd been stuck in for years. **"If you don't learn the lesson you're meant to learn,"** she told him, **"you stay in the same stage of growth.** Even if the people or places change, the same problems will follow you."

The dysfunction will just take on new faces—repeating in friendships, relationships, jobs, and family dynamics—until you finally face what's inside. You can't bypass the chrysalis. That hardened shell of old habits, fears, and defense mechanisms doesn't just fall away on its own. **You have to do the inner work: recognize the pattern, release the baggage, shift your mindset, and then break through.** A quote I recently read put it eloquently: *"The pattern isn't the enemy... it's the invitation. You'll keep walking the same loop until you realize you're holding the key."* That's how transformation happens. Only then can you truly fly.

Strength Training for the Soul

Around the same time, I started working with a personal trainer. I had focused for years on cardio—burning fat, trying to become lean—but she quickly pointed out something I'd been overlooking: strength training. Especially core strength. Without it, she warned, we grow weaker over time—less stable, more prone to injury, and quicker to fatigue.

She introduced me to planks, boat holds, and dead bugs—

exercises with almost no movement, but intense concentration. "Strengthen your core," she said, "and everything else improves—your posture, balance, and energy."

She wasn't just talking about the body. The same is true for life.

When your inner core is strong, you meet life's chaos with calm and strength. You set boundaries without guilt. You lead with love instead of fear. You stay grounded when others wobble. You parent from a deep well of peace and clarity.

And when you stray—as we all do—you know how to find your way back.

QUESTIONS TO JOURNAL

- What is your personal North Star? When you lose your way, how do you return to it?
- What parts of yourself feel strong? Which areas need attention, nourishment, or healing?
- What would it look like to strengthen the core of your being—spiritually, emotionally, physically—one small step at a time?

As the Zen proverb goes: **"Obstacles do not block the path; they are the path."**

Seize Your Power

Moms, I hope you now see the full range of powers available to you. With them, you can parent from strength rather than control, draw from your inner wisdom and higher power to navigate challenges, and lead your family with greater presence and intention. You've learned how to let go of ego, deepen connection, and bring out the best in those you love. You've begun to create a home grounded in faith, love, and the belief in everyday miracles.

And just as important, you've discovered how to harness the power to launch—not only your children—but yourself.

But perhaps most profoundly, you've realized this journey—this sacred, wild, and often heartbreaking path of parenting—isn't only about raising your children.

It's about raising yourself.

And when you do that…

You don't just give them wings.

You grow your own.

> **See all women as mothers,
> serve them as your mother.
> When you see the entire world as
> the mother, the ego falls away.**
>
> —Neem Karoli Baba

REFERENCES AND RESOURCES
Self Help, Spirituality, and Life Purpose

The Holy Bible: 1611 edition, King James Version

A New Earth: Awakening to Your Life's Purpose by Eckhart Tolle (Penguin, 2005)

The Path Made Clear: Discovering Your Life's Direction and Purpose by Oprah Winfrey (Flatiron Books, 2019)

The Power of Now: A Guide to Spiritual Enlightenment by Eckhart Tolle (Namaste Publishing, 1997)

The Seven Spiritual Laws of Success: A Practical Guide to the Fulfillment of Your Dreams by Deepak Chopra (New World Library, 1994)

Parenting

Failure to Launch: Why Your Twentysomething Hasn't Grown Up... and What to Do About It by Mark McConville (G. P. Putnam's Sons, 2020)

How to Raise an Adult: Break Free of the Overparenting Trap and Prepare Your Kid for Success by Julie Lythcott-Haims (Henry Holt and Company, 2015)

ScreamFree Parenting: The Revolutionary Approach to Raising Your Kids Without Losing Your Cool by Hal Edward Runkel, LMFT (Broadway Books, 2007)

The Awakened Family: How to Raise Empowered, Resilient, and Conscious Children by Shefali Tsabary, Ph. D. (Penguin Books; Reprint Edition, 2017)

Coaching

Parenting Modern Teens, Sean Donohue and Sean Potts https://www.parentingmodernteens.com

WisdomBCoaching,   https://wisdombcoaching.com

About the Author

Wisdom B. Fields is a mother and a coach. She is a graduate of MIT and Stanford and has had a successful career as a product management executive. As a trained life coach, she focuses on helping mothers, mid-level managers, and product leaders discover their own power to bring about change in themselves, the workplace, and their homes. She currently lives in the San Francisco Bay Area with her husband and three children.

For more information or to sign up for coaching, please visit

http://WisdomBcoaching.com

www.ingramcontent.com/pod-product-compliance
Lightning Source LLC
Chambersburg PA
CBHW020529080526
44583CB00013B/789